CHRISTIAN NON-DUALISM

A COMMENTARY ON THEOLOGIA GERMANICA

CHRISTIAN NON-DUALISM

A COMMENTARY ON THEOLOGIA GERMANICA

SWAMI NIRMALANANDA GIRI
(ABBOT GEORGE BURKE)

LIGHT OF THE SPIRIT
PRESS
CEDAR CREST, NEW MEXICO

Published by
Light of the Spirit Press
lightofthespiritpress.com

Light of the Spirit Monastery
P. O. Box 1370
Cedar Crest, New Mexico 87008
OCOY.org

ISBN: 978-1-955046-34-3 (paperback)
       978-1-955046-35-0 (ebook)

Library of Congress Control Number: 2025910383
Light of the Spirit Press, Cedar Crest, New Mexico

    Bisac categories:
1. OCC012000 BODY, MIND & SPIRIT / Mysticism
2. REL047000 RELIGION / Mysticism
3. REL067000 RELIGION / Christian Theology / General
First edition, (June 2025)

12042025

CONTENTS

INTRODUCTION

The book known now as *Theologia Germanica* was originally called simply *The Frankfurter* [*Der Franckforter*], the author being a priest and a member of the Teutonic Order living in Frankfurt, Germany in the later fourteenth century. And that is all we know about him.

Nearly two hundred editions of *Theologia Germanica* were published in the Christian West between the sixteenth and twentieth centuries. Naturally, it had its opponents. John Calvin wrote to his followers in Frankfurt that it is "conceived by Satan's cunning... it contains a hidden poison which can poison the church." In 1612, Pope Paul V placed it on the Catholic Church's *Index Librorum Prohibitorum* where it remained. But Catholic mystics continued to read the book anyway.

Considering that there was no contact with India or Indian philosophy at the time *Theologia Germanica* was written, it is proof that the non-dual view of God and man can arise within any religious environment which includes mysticism and mystical theology such as that when Christianity in Europe was undivided and experiencing the spiritual character of the Age of Faith.

Certainly the Frankfurter heard the assurance of Christ: "Behold, I have set before thee an open door, and no man can shut it" (Revelation 3:8).

I have only commented on the first thirty-eight chapters since the remaining six chapters are polemics aimed at various theological speculations current at the priest-knight's time and are irrelevant to us at this point in time.

The translation used in this commentary is that of Susanna Winkworth.

The Perfect and Perfection

(From Chapter One)

St. Paul says, "When that which is perfect is come, then that which is in part shall be done away." (I Corinthians 13:10). Now mark what is "that which is perfect," and "that which is in part."

The author is going to define "perfect" for us, but first a look at the Biblical text is appropriate. The Greek word in the New Testament translated "perfect" is *teleios*, which means something that is complete, lacking nothing, with the implication of being beyond improvement, the state of ultimate completion. Beyond it there is nothing. It is the end, the pinnacle of a journey or a process such as evolution. It is Unity Absolute. It is exactly what is meant by the Sanskrit word *Purna*—total, full, complete, which is what our English term "perfect" used to mean, rather than just "without fault." When something is *purna*, it is the whole thing. There is nothing else beside it.

"That which is perfect" is a Being, who has comprehended and included all things in Himself and His own Substance, and without whom, and beside whom, there is no true Substance, and in whom all things have their Substance.

God is absolutely perfect and is the perfection of all that (truly) exists, just as God alone is the absolute good, and the goodness of all that exists according to the Lord Jesus himself: "There is none good but one, that is, God" (Matthew 19:17). But it is necessary to consider what is implied as well as what is directly stated. This is especially true in Eastern texts, and the Frankfurter is centered in the same non-dual vision as the sages

1

of India. This sentence sets forth the following fundamental truths about God and existence itself:

1) God encompasses and includes all things in himself, in his very being.

2) Everything that exists consists of the very substance of God.

(These two statements can be restated as: God is everything and everything is God.)

3) Nothing exists beside God.

4) Nothing exists outside God.

5) God is self-existent.

6) Everything draws its existence from God.

7) God is eternal.

8) All things are eternal in their essence or substance which is God.

9) The manifested form of all things is non-eternal, having a beginning and an end.

> **For he is the Substance of all things, and is in himself unchangeable and immoveable, and changes and moves all things else.**

Therefore everything that takes place is the action of God, either directly or through power borrowed or drawn from him. Consequently God is the sole Actor in the final analysis. This is why the Bhagavad Gita teaches that the man of wisdom knows that he never does anything of himself. "'I do not do anything;' thus thinks the steadfast knower of truth while seeing, hearing, touching, smelling, eating, walking, sleeping, breathing, speaking, releasing, and holding, opening and closing his eyes" (5:8-9).

> **But "that which is in part," or the Imperfect, is that which has its source in, or springs from the Perfect; just as a brightness or a visible appearance flows out from the sun or a candle, and appears to be somewhat, this or that. And it is called a creature; and of all these "things which are in part," none is the Perfect. So also the Perfect is none of the things which are in part.**

God is the Absolute, all else is only relative. The Frankfurter therefore always refers to relativity as "the Imperfect" because of itself it is nothing. Nevertheless all things are sacred because they draw their existence, even if only momentarily, from him who is the Holy God, Holy Mighty, Holy Immortal.

In these few sentences the Teutonic Priest has presented the concept of Maya and shown it to be completely compatible with authentic Christianity.

But "that which is in part," or the Imperfect, is that which has its source in, or springs from the Perfect; just as a brightness or a visible appearance flows out from the sun or a candle, and appears to be somewhat, this or that. The implication here is the classical principle that all things are mere appearances only, being the Real Itself under a momentary, false appearance. This may sound too abstract to unravel, but it is not. All creation is but the dream of God, the Cosmic Dreamer, and that we are dreamers along with and within him. God is dreaming the cosmos and we are dreaming our lives within his dream. The purpose of this dreaming is the development and evolution of our finite consciousness within his infinite consciousness.

Our many lives (reincarnations) are dreams within the dream, and in that sense definitely real, but not as they appear to be. We dream mortality but are always immortal; we dream materiality but are always spirit. It is a pretend game of the children of God so they can come to share in the life and consciousness of the Father. (See *Robe of Light*.)

And it is called a creature; and of all these "things which are in part," none is the Perfect. So also the Perfect is none of the things which are in part. When we enter a motion picture theater before the program there is a large white screen in the front. But when the program starts, we do not see the screen at all but the moving pictures from the projector. When the program is over there is the screen just as before. Consciousness (spirit) is the screen on which creation is seen. Like the motion picture, the creation is light which appears and disappears. If the screen was not there, no matter how much the projection might run we would see nothing but vague patterns of light. In the same way creation exists only in relation to the Creator. Yet the Creator is not the creation and the creation is not the Creator. The creation depends on the Creator, while the Creator depends on nothing. Actually the creation hides the Creator on which it depends.

The Bhagavad Gita explains that everything is prakriti–energy which essentially is light. Just as certain kinds of color projection consist of three primary colors in innumerable combinations, so the creation (prakriti) consists of the modes of energy called "gunas." There are three gunas: sattwa, rajas and tamas. So in the Gita God tells us: "Know that sattwic, rajasic and tamasic states of being proceed from me. *But I am not in them–they are in me.* All this world is deluded by the three states produced by the gunas. It does not perceive me, who am higher than these and eternal" (Bhagavad Gita 7:12-13).

Just as we believe in the motion picture, reacting with emotions and momentarily feeling as though the figures and incidents on the screen are real, feeling fear, disgust, indignation, admiration and awe, laughing and crying–all according to the kind of movie we are witnessing–so we believe in the creation-movie, much more than we do in the Creator. In fact, those utterly absorbed in the creation movie often disbelieve and vigorously oppose the idea of the Creator. Many disbelieve in God when they are immersed and forgetful in the realm of relative existence, which is no permanent existence at all.

A dream exists as a psychic experience, but is not real. Yet it does exist at the moment. In the same way the creation exists, but only in the minds of God and sentient beings. Ultimately only God and the spirits within God are real, dreaming together for the development of the spirits. Just as in *A Christmas Carol* Scrooge's heart is changed by his three dreams, so we are being changed by the dreams we call our lives.

Western people reading in Indian philosophy often assume that "unreal" means non-existent, when it often means that the way a thing is seen is not real but a misperception of an actual reality. For a while relativity exists, but only as a dream. You and I can sit and daydream and create a world and populate it with people whose appearance and action we imagine complete with color, sound and physical sensation. But it never at any times is real. We are what is real about it all. And it is the same with God and creation.

The things which are in part can be apprehended, known, and expressed; but the Perfect cannot be apprehended, known, or expressed by any creature as creature.

The ancient sages of India knew by direct experience of Brahman that nothing can be said about It as the ultimate Reality, not even that It exists, since our only experience and concept of existence is that of relative things. Therefore they said that all we can say about It is *Neti Neti*: Not This, Not That. The earliest Fathers of the Christian Church said exactly this same thing in what is known as apophatic theology. Only by direct union with God can God be known. And even then it will not be through the mind or intellect, so therefore nothing can be said about God. The second clause: "The Perfect cannot be apprehended, known, or expressed by any creature as creature," means that if we cease to be a creature, a relative being trapped in Maya, we can apprehend and know God. But we have to become god ourselves–realize our divine essence, finite though it may be–to do so. And even then we cannot say a word about him.

Therefore we do not give a name to the Perfect, for it is none of these. The creature as creature cannot know nor apprehend it, name nor conceive it.

All "names" of God in the religions of the world are really descriptive titles, and essentially do not designate God in a "proper" or exclusive manner as they all have meanings of their own, such as almighty, universal, and suchlike.

By "name" the author of *Theologia Germanica* means a defining term that truly expresses what God is. We can "name" anything in relative existence, but God transcends relativity so he cannot really even be spoken about in the highest sense. Nevertheless we need to speak about God because he is the Sole Reality. So we use our human terms since that is all we possess, but we must always realize that we are not really able to say anything about God: not even that he exists. As a consequence we should not dogmatize about God and wish to impose our dogmas on others. All we can say about God are hints: intuition must take over from there. We cannot define or comprehend God intellectually, but we can know him through direct experience of him in the depths of our own being. When we know ourselves, we know God, for "I and my Father are One" (John 10:30).

> **"Now when that which is Perfect is come, then that which is in part shall be done away." But when does it come? I say, when as much as may be, it is known, felt and tasted of the soul.**

Those spirits which are sufficiently purified and evolved can know, feel and experience the infinite, though themselves finite. This is the fundamental purpose of creation and their entry into it. (Again, see *Robe of Light*.) But when will they be purified and evolved enough for this to take place? That is totally in their hands. God has already done everything necessary in the projection and supervision of the creation; the rest is up to them. They and they alone will decide when the Great Moment will come. But first the entire situation must be completely under their control. Wishing, aspiring, praying, affirming and rousing up the will, emotions and intellect can accomplish nothing but further delusion and bondage.

Yoga and yoga alone is the means of control and ultimate mastery. The aspirant must become a yogi, a proficient—and therefore self-sufficient—practitioner of the supreme science of yoga. From that moment onward it is all according to the yogi's application and diligence. Because this is so, in the Yoga Sutras (1:20) Patanjali tells us that the yogi must have developed the effective faith, energy, understanding and high intelligence necessary for the attainment of samadhi. (For samadhi is not the end but the beginning of actual yoga.) Then he says that "it [samadhi] is nearest to those whose desire [for samadhi] is intensely strong" (v. 21). But that of itself is not enough. Effort must be put forth. So he continues: "A further differentiation [arises] by reason of the mild, medium and intense [nature of means employed]" (v. 22). And finally: "By total giving of the life to God" (v. 23). As the Gita affirms: "In this matter there is a single, resolute understanding" (Bhagavad Gita 2:41): the absolute necessity for

God-realization. The Gita speaks of "steady insight in meditation" (Bhagavad Gita 2:44).

Now, considering all these necessary prerequisites, how many successful yogis do we think there will be? Krishna says in the Gita: "Of thousands of human beings scarcely anyone at all strives for perfection, and of those adept in that striving, scarcely anyone knows me in truth" (Bhagavad Gita 7:3). Saint Paul said it this way: "Know ye not that they which run in a race run all, but one receiveth the prize? So run, that ye may obtain" (I Corinthians 9:24). Those who do not approach yoga with this understanding and the requisite commitment as well as the strength of mind and heart to carry it all through are destined to fail.

> **For the lack lies altogether in us, and not in it. In like manner the sun lights the whole world, and is as near to one as another, yet a blind man sees it not; but the fault thereof lies in the blind man, not in the sun.**

By "lack" two kinds of deficiency are meant. One is simple limitation. We do not fly because we have no wings and cannot live underwater because we have no gills. There is no fault in this. But the other is limitation and lack from making no effort to extend our limitation because we consider it too much trouble or simply have no interest in it at all. We live surrounded by people who never give God or spiritual life a thought. They will think about flying to the moon before thinking about God or spiritual life. In some this is a no-fault matter of lack of evolution, and in others a sign of conscious negativity and aversion to higher consciousness and God the Highest.

As already pointed out, there is no lack on God's part, for the very presence of creation is evidence of his doing all to help us onward in evolution. As Yogananda once pointed out, we already have God's blessing, but we lack our blessing for spiritual life. "One should uplift oneself by the lower self; one should not degrade oneself. The lower self can truly be a friend of the lower self, and the lower self alone can be an enemy of the lower self. For him who has conquered himself by the lower self, the lower self is a friend. But for him who has not conquered himself, the lower self remains hostile, like an enemy" (Bhagavad Gita 6:5-6).

Through his omnipresence God is near to every single person "that they should seek the Lord, if haply they might feel after him, and find him, though he be not far from every one of us: For in him we live, and move, and have our being: For we are also his offspring" (Acts 17:27-28). Nothing can be closer to us than God. Some people are like compasses with sensitive needles that point always to God; others are like compasses with weak needles that sometimes do and sometimes do not point to God; and others are like compasses with needles that never point to God. Believe it or not, when I was a Boy Scout I bought a cheap compass that never pointed north and after a while consistently pointed south. I have met a lot of people in my life whose inner compass was always turned away from God, sometimes intentionally and sometimes not intentionally, but the result was the same.

When I was in my teens, an elderly man who was known to have a very weak heart came to work on our television set. When he was done he asked my father to play something for him on our organ. I never heard my father play anything but hymns, and this was no exception. But before half a minute had passed the man said to him: "You can save that for when I am laid out." So my father stopped playing and the man went home and was dead and "laid out" in four days. Many ignore God, but many have an aversion to God. Our spiritual state and destiny lie in our will alone. Few things are sillier than the "why does God allow?" demand. It is because we have been given freedom by God that can be used or misused. It is all up to us.

> **And like as the sun may not hide its brightness, but must give light unto the earth (for heaven indeed draws its light and heat from another fountain), so also God, who is the highest Good, wills not to hide himself from any, wheresoever he finds a devout soul, that is thoroughly purified from all creatures.**

A lot of people like to accuse God of "hiding" from or "abandoning" them, but Saint Paul assures us: "If we believe not, yet he abideth faithful:

he cannot deny himself" (II Timothy 2:13). As Yogananda said once in a talk: "He never denies us; we deny him." That is the truth. It is God's nature to draw us upward into his "throne," into his perfect Being and Consciousness which he wills to share with us. That is why he told Abraham: "I am thy shield, and thy exceeding great reward." (Genesis 15:1). And if we do not violate our nature as eternally existing in God, we will cooperate in rising to him.

As the Frankfurter says, God is looking for "a devout soul, that is thoroughly purified from all creatures," one who is completely free from desire and attachment for things of either earth or heaven, intent instead on complete liberation of spirit. Krishna describes such a one in this way: "Among the virtuous, four kinds seek me: the distressed, the seekers of knowledge, the seekers of wealth and the wise. Of them, the wise man, ever united, devoted to the One, is pre-eminent. Exceedingly dear am I to the man of wisdom, and he is dear to me. All these indeed are exalted, but I see the man of wisdom as my very Self. He, with mind steadfast, abides in me, the Supreme Goal" (Bhagavad Gita 7:16-18).

> **For in what measure we put off the creature, in the same measure are we able to put on the Creator; neither more nor less.**

Since the human being is really a god in embryonic form, it is possible for people to divest themselves of humanity and all forms of relative existence, even those of the highest worlds. And the less a person is part of creation, the more he is assumed into the Being of the Creator. He does not become the Creator, but he "puts on" the Creator, being clothed in divinity, sharing in the qualities and powers of God insofar as a finite being can do so. That is why Saint Paul speaks of "putting on Christ" (Romans 13:14; Galatians 3:27.) It is the nature of every individual spirit (jiva) to attain divinity. "Jesus answered them, Is it not written in your law, I said, Ye are gods?" (John 10:34). This was a teaching of original Christianity, and still is a teaching of authentic Christianity. As I explained to more than one missionary in India, the Hindus, Buddhists and Taoists are far more truly Christian than they are. That is why Jesus said of people like those missionaries: "Many will say to me in that day, Lord, Lord, have we not prophesied in thy name? and in thy name have cast out devils? and in thy name done many wonderful works? And then will I profess unto them, I never knew you: depart from me, ye that work iniquity." (Matthew 7:22-23). Their religion itself is iniquity, and is not of Christ or God. As Jesus further said to such false teachers who claim to be "winning souls" for God and Christ: "Woe unto you, hypocrites! for ye compass sea and land to make one proselyte, and when he is made, ye make him twofold more the child of hell than yourselves." (Matthew 23:15).

For if mine eye is to see anything, it must be single, or else be purified from all other things.

"The light of the body is the eye: if therefore thine eye be single, thy whole body shall be full of light." (Matthew 6:22; Luke 11:34).

Now the priest-knight brings it home to the individual, including himself. For anyone to experience union with God, the "eye" of the intellect, known in Sanskrit as the buddhi (intelligence factor of the mind), must be capable of that experience. The Greek word translated "eye" in the New Testament is *ophthalmos*, which means both the physical eye and the mental eye–the faculty of perception and knowledge. This faculty must be single: *haplous*, which means simple and single in the sense of whole: totally operational. One of the roots of *haplous* is *pleko*, which means gathered up into one. So the single eye is the same as the "one-pointed" mind of the adept yogi. "This is the Supreme Being, attained by one-pointed devotion alone" (Bhagavad Gita 8:22). "Has this been heard by you with a one-pointed mind?" (Bhagavad Gita 18:72). "When he is absorbed in the Self alone, with mind controlled, free from longing, from all desires, then he is known to be steadfast. As a lamp in a windless place flickers not: to such is compared the yogi of controlled mind, performing the yoga of the Self. He knows that endless joy which is apprehended by the buddhi beyond the senses; and established in that he does not deviate from the truth. Let this dissolution of union with pain be known as yoga. This yoga is to be practiced with determination, with an assured mind" (Bhagavad Gita 6:18-19, 21, 23).

All "things" must be emptied from the mind in meditation, and most of the time outside meditation, too.

Where heat and light enter in, cold and darkness must needs depart; it cannot be otherwise.

Now this is the bedrock fact: the more God enters into our life, the more everything else that is not God must either depart or be transmuted into divine nature. The creation comes from the Creator, but as far as sentient beings are concerned "creature" and Creator become antithetical at one stage of their evolution, because from that point onward they must increasingly become god and decrease as human. This is the highest sense of Saint John the Baptist's declaration: "He must increase, but I must decrease" (John 3:30). The "I" is not the true Self, the Atman, but the ego (ahankara) the false self. This can only be, as the Frankfurter says, "it cannot be otherwise" because truth cannot coexist with falsehood in the same place. In each one of us the creature (artificial) nature must decrease and the eternal, divine nature increase. "For what fellowship hath righteousness with unrighteousness? and what communion hath light with darkness?" (II Corinthians 6:14).

The quote from Saint Paul at the beginning of *Theologia Germanica* speaks of the imperfect or partial being "done away." The Greek word for that is *katargeo*, which means to abolish or dissolve something absolutely, leaving no residue. It also means to be loosed from bonds, to be delivered. So it means just the same as the Sanskrit word for salvation: moksha–liberation. It has the implication of rendering something completely inoperative. Therefore Saint John said: "Whosoever is born of God doth not commit sin; for his seed remaineth in him: and he cannot sin, because he is born of God" (I John 3:9).

But one might say, "Now since the Perfect cannot be known nor apprehended of any creature, but the soul is a creature, how

> can it be known by the soul?" Answer: This is why we say, "by
> the soul as a creature." We mean it is impossible to the creature
> in virtue of its creature-nature and qualities, that by which it
> says "I" and "myself."

As already indicated previously, the less we are a creature and the more
we are a spirit like the Creator, the more we can know God. But this also
opens up another aspect to spiritual life: Does our religion, our religious
involvement, come from our spirit or our ego? When the ego is the basis
of our religious life and practice, then only confusion, delusion and harm
will result. Since the ego is our personal "Satan," it truly is "all hell" that
will break loose, because it is totally inimical to God. Only to the degree
that we are estranged (separated) from the world, can we enter into communion with God. "Know ye not that the friendship of the world is enmity
with God? whosoever therefore will be a friend of the world is the enemy
of God." (James 4:4).

We must put off our humanity and put on divinity. This is not really
hard, because humanity is not our real nature, but divinity is.

> For in whatsoever creature the Perfect shall be known, there-
> in creature-nature, qualities, the I, the Self and the like, must all
> be lost and done away. This is the meaning of that saying of St.
> Paul: "When that which is perfect is come" (that is, when it is
> known), "then that which is in part" (to wit, creature-nature,
> qualities, the I, the Self, the Mine) will be despised and counted
> for nought.

(Please keep in mind that when the author says "Self" he means the
ego in the sense of self-centeredness; but when I say "Self" I mean our
divine Spirit that is always one with God.)

All the saints I have known in East and West were obviously not of
this world, but citizens of the heaven-world. They all had that trait in
common, and intensely so. Jesus said of himself: "I am not of this world"
(John 8:23). And of his disciples: "Ye are not of the world, but I have

chosen you out of the world" (John 15:19). "Love not the world, neither the things that are in the world. If any man love the world, the love of the Father is not in him. For all that is in the world, the lust of the flesh, and the lust of the eyes, and the pride of life, is not of the Father, but is of the world" (I John 2:15-16). "Yea doubtless, and I count all things but loss for the excellency of the knowledge of Christ Jesus my Lord: for whom I have suffered the loss of all things, and do count them but dung, that I may win Christ, and be found in him" (Philippians 3:8-9).

The word translated "loss" is *zemia*, which means loss and damage, the idea being that the world causes us to lose the awareness of our true Self and of God, the Self of our Self. Further, it damages and even destroys us by our very involvement in it. We should not just be disinterested in the world, considering it worthless, we should realize that it can destroy us, spiritually speaking. This world is not just a place of death, it produces death in those that let it do so, who mistakenly seek only the false life of the world, thinking it is true life. Jesus told his disciples: "I have overcome the world" (John 16:33), so they would understand that they must do the same. We are not to hate or fear the world, but we must overcome it by uprooting it from our hearts.

The word translated "dung" is *skubalon*, which means excrement (*kuon*, the excrement of dogs). This should be our understanding of the world. Not that we should be seized with hatred or disgust for the world, but that we should keep ourselves from it and turn wholeheartedly to God, loving God above (and instead of) all. The "due" we should pay the world is absolutely nothing, for God is All.

"The world" I am speaking about is not the world of God's making, but the world defiled and distorted by ignorance and evil, the false world of corrupted humanity.

> **So long as we think much of these things, cleave to them with love, joy, pleasure or desire, so long remains the Perfect unknown to us.**

This needs no comment, only heeding and following.

> But it might further be said, "You say, beside the Perfect there is no Substance, yet say again that somewhat flows out from it: now is not that which has flowed out from it, something beside it."
>
> Answer: This is why we say, beside it, or without it, there is no true Substance.
>
> That which has flowed forth from it, is no true Substance, and has no Substance except in the Perfect, but is an accident, or a brightness, or a visible appearance, which is no Substance, and has no Substance except in the fire whence the brightness flowed forth, such as the sun or a candle.

Realizing the dream-nature of the world, we can understand these two paragraphs. The projection-creation of the world is an emanation from Brahman the Absolute, just as the early Christian writer Tertullian explained that the Son and the Holy Spirit are really emanations of the Father. Never does God lose his status as One, Only, Without a Second: Ekam, Evam, Adwitiyam (Chandogya Upanishad 6.2.1). Yet all these emanations both *of* and *from* God are merely ideations of the Divine Mind. They have no objective reality apart from God. As ideas they are things and do exist, but they never at any time are real in the sense that God and our spirits are real. For only that which is eternal is real, all else is momentary. Yet since they are emanations or radiations of God they possess an essential divine or godlike character. When seen as what they really are, the illumined individual lives in God and God alone while others stumble through life after life, in a sense blinded by the Light. Not only is the creation momentary, a dream, so also is the Creator, Ishwara the Only Begotten of the Father. So also is the creative power, the Holy Breath, the Holy Spirit. There never is anything but the One at any time, the One that encompasses the many that exist within him from eternity.

Ella Wheeler Wilcox wrote:

God and I in space alone
and nobody else in view.
"And where are the people, O Lord," I said,
"the earth below and the sky o'er head
and the dead whom once I knew?"

"That was a dream," God smiled and said,
"A dream that seemed to be true.
There were no people, living or dead,
there was no earth, and no sky o'er head;
there was only Myself–in you."

"Why do I feel no fear," I asked,
"meeting You here this way?
For I have sinned I know full well–
and is there heaven, and is there hell,
and is this the Judgment Day?"

"Nay, those were but dreams,"
the Great God said,
"Dreams that have ceased to be.
There are no such things as fear or sin;
there is no you–you never have been–
there is nothing at all
but Me."

SIN AND SATAN

(FROM CHAPTER TWO)

The Scripture and the Faith and the Truth say, Sin is nought else, but that the creature turns away from the unchangeable Good and betakes itself to the changeable; that is to say, that it turns away from the Perfect to "that which is in part" and imperfect, and most often to itself.

The Greek word translated "sin" in the New Testament is *amartia*, which means to lack something, to miss the mark, to be in error. "Sins" are deficiencies, shortcomings (falling short of the ideal), illusions and delusions. Sin, then, is a state, and the actions of someone in that state are the symptoms of sin: sinful, but not sin itself. This being so, the idea of being forgiven or pardoned for sins comes from a misunderstanding of the nature of sin. We do not need to be forgiven, we need to rise from the condition of mind and heart that is the state of sin. Then we will commit no more sinful acts. The necessity is to be freed from sin and its effects. Jesus said: "Whosoever committeth sin is the servant of sin." (John 8:34). But he also said: "Ye shall know the truth, and the truth shall make you free" (John 8:32) from sin.

When we understand sin in this way then we realize that we need a profound change in our consciousness, not just learning and following a behavioral code the way an animal learns and performs tricks.

According to the Teutonic priest, sin is the condition of being turned away from God and focussed on something else. Leaving the unchangeable God we plunge into the ever-changing tides of the sea of samsara. We suffer and enmesh ourselves further in samsara in the vain attempt to alleviate our suffering. It never occurs to us to get out of samsara, because we are so deceived by it we do not think there is anything else. We even come to assume that leaving samsara is to enter a state of annihilation. So we cling desperately to bondage, ignorance, and illusion: to the condition of sin. This causes us to become obsessed with our egoic existence, centered on it completely and seeing all things as they relate to our ego, our false Self.

> **Now mark: when the creature claims for its own anything good, such as Substance, Life, Knowledge, Power, and in short whatever we should call good, as if it were that, or possessed that, or that were itself, or that proceeded from it–as often as this comes to pass, the creature goes astray.**

We do not naturally outgrow sin, but become further and further bound to and in it because we misunderstand it.

The root of all our problems is the illusion of separate existence from God, the belief that we are self-existent and self-sufficient, that there is such a thing as existence apart from God. Consequently we believe that we possess something as our "own" or "us." Therefore as the author says, when we say of anything "that is mine" we are leading ourselves astray, further into bondage and blindness. Everything we think we have really belongs to God. We are living within God and drawing from God everything, because he is existence itself. He shares himself with us, but everything is really his, and that includes us. "For in him we live, and move, and have our being" (Acts 17:28). Non-duality is the only truth because non-duality is the nature of God and of ourselves.

> **What did the devil do else, or what was his going astray and his fall else, but that he claimed for himself to be also somewhat, and would have it that somewhat was his, and somewhat was due to him? This setting up of a claim and his I and Me and Mine, these were his going astray, and his fall. And thus it is to this day.**

"How art thou fallen from heaven, O Lucifer, son of the morning! how art thou cut down to the ground, which didst weaken the nations!

For thou hast said in thine heart, I will ascend into heaven, I will exalt my throne above the stars of God: I will sit also upon the mount of the congregation, in the sides of the north: I will ascend above the heights of the clouds; I will be like the most High" (Isaiah 14:12-14).

Lucifer aspired to attain the highest level in all the worlds and equality with God. But he misunderstood them completely, thinking that they were matters of personal, egoic power and glory rather than expressions of an infinite nature which he could never possess. If he had aspired to purify himself so as to be one with God in loving and serving God and all sentient beings, he would have succeeded. Instead his own distorted mind and ambitions impelled him downward rather than upward.

It is important to realize that he cast himself down; God did not do so. Creation being essentially consciousness, it responds to each individual person's state of mind and heart. The idea that God is arbitrarily lifting up and casting down those that please or displease him is not just wrong, it is a blasphemy. For by the faculty of free will which God never violates, each one of us is rising and falling according to our own will exclusively.

Again, the universe is living consciousness and responds to the consciousness of each individual being within it. In one sense God is never a potentate or ruler of the cosmos: we are. But we would rather blame him for the consequences of our actions. For example, the false idea is that we are rewarded or punished by God in response to an action, when in reality it is we ourselves that lift up and cast down ourselves. Karma is a matter of action and reaction. The creation is a mirror in which our face is shown to us. Here is the truth about it all: "All this world is deluded by the three states produced by the gunas. It does not perceive me, who am higher than these and eternal" (Bhagavad Gita 7:13). "These acts do not bind me, sitting as one apart, indifferent and unattached in these actions. With me as overseer Prakriti produces both the animate and the inanimate; because of this the world revolves" (Bhagavad Gita 9:9-10) "The Lord does not create either means of action or action itself in this world, nor the union of action with its fruit. On the other hand, the swabhava impels one to action. The Omnipresent takes note of neither demerit nor merit. Knowledge is enveloped by ignorance; as a result of that people are deluded. But those in whom this ignorance of the Self has been destroyed by knowledge–that knowledge of theirs, like the sun, reveals the Supreme Brahman. Those whose minds are absorbed in That, whose Selves are fixed on That, whose foundation is That, who hold That as the highest object, whose evils have been shaken off by knowledge, attain the ending of rebirth" (Bhagavad Gita 5:14-17). As usual, the Bhagavad Gita expresses it perfectly.

Though made in the image of God, we have reshaped ourselves into images of Lucifer through our personal Lucifer, the ego. That is why Jesus said: "Ye are of your father the devil, and the lusts of your father ye will do. He was a murderer from the beginning, and abode not in the truth, because there is no truth in him. When he speaketh a lie, he speaketh of his own: for he is a liar, and the father of it." (John 8:44).

According to the preceding verse the luciferic personality has these traits: 1) domination by egocentric desires; 2) suppression of the true self in exaltation of the false ego-self; 3) insistence on being what one is not and never can be; 4) living according to egoic fantasies instead of realities; 5) denial and rejection of any realities that conflict with the egoic mind. Such a person is a kind of self-homicidal maniac.

"Evil-doers (wrongdoers), the lowest (vilest; worst) of men, bereft of knowledge by maya, do not resort to (seek) me, being attached to (existing within) a demonic mode of existence" (Bhagavad Gita 7:15). This is a terrible condition, but one that results completely from the individual's own choice and efforts of will. Those who think they are too advanced for religion like to toss off such statements as: "We all create our own heaven or hell right here on earth." Yes; that is true. And if they really believed or understood what they say they would be very different persons than they are.

Fall and Restoration

(Chapter Three)

Keeping in mind the words about the fall of Lucifer in the previous chapter, the Frankfurter considers us who, though made in the image of God, have chosen to mutate ourselves into images of Lucifer.

> **What else did Adam do but this same thing? It is said, it was because Adam ate the apple that he was lost, or fell. I say, it was because of his claiming something for his own, and because of his I, Mine, Me, and the like. Had he eaten seven apples, and yet never claimed anything for his own, he would not have fallen: but as soon as he called something his own, he fell, and would have fallen if he had never touched an apple.**

It was not an action that brought about the banishment of Adam and Eve from Paradise, but their minds which were oriented toward the ego and not toward either God or their true spirit-being. Thinking we can make anything ours is a universal delusion. Life after life death takes everything away from us but our minds and spirit. Yet, instead of cultivating them and orienting them toward God who is their very essence, we keep grabbing for the mirage of relative existence.

When I was just a child I somehow had the idea that if I saw something in a dream that I wanted and held on to it, when I awoke I would have brought it over from my dream. Woolworth's Dime Store was my Paradise, and I used to dream that I was in it all alone, going through the whole store and gathering up whatever I wanted. Then I would sit down on the floor and hug everything to my chest as hard as I could. I would close my eyes tight and put all my attention on holding to my loot. The very intense focus of my mind would wake me up. I would look and find that it had not worked. It took quite a few dreams before I figured out that it would never work, that dream was not reality. Some years later I learned that not even the dream of my waking hours was real.

"I, Mine, Me" are the thieves that steal everything from us life after life as we pursue the mirages that we only desire because they are delusions of our flawed minds and hearts. Awakening from such a dream is no easy matter. "Truly this maya of mine made of the gunas is difficult to go beyond" (Bhagavad Gita 7:14).

> **Behold! I have fallen a hundred times more often and deeply, and gone a hundred times farther astray than Adam; and not all mankind could mend his fall, or bring him back from going astray. But how shall my fall be amended? It must be healed as Adam's fall was healed, and on the self-same wise. By whom, and on what wise was that healing brought to pass? Mark this: man could not without God, and God should not without man. Wherefore God took human nature or manhood upon himself and was made man, and man was made divine. Thus the healing was brought to pass.**

God cannot restore a fallen human being without the agency, the will and cooperation of that human. And a fallen human being cannot be restored without the agency of God. The work of restoration can only come about by both God and man working together. "For we are labourers together with God" (I Corinthians 3:9). "We then, as workers together with him, beseech you also that ye receive not the grace of God in vain" (II Corinthians 6:1). "Wherefore, my beloved,… work out your own salvation…. For it is God which worketh in you both to will and to do of his good pleasure" (Philippians 2:12-13).

We must strive to divest ourselves of creaturehood (which includes the state of humanity) so that God can assume us into himself and deify us—yet with the distinction between him and us left intact. This transmutation was revealed in Jesus, not to just be a marvel to us, but to be an example and pattern for us to follow. That which God did in him can and must be done in us. "Unto you it is given to know the mystery of the kingdom of God" (Mark 4:11). "For in him dwelleth all the fulness of the Godhead bodily" (Colossians 2:9), and the same indwelling can occur in us. "Behold, I shew you a mystery; We shall not all sleep, but we shall all be changed," (I Corinthians 15:51) in the resurrection: not of the body but of the spirit when God says to each one of us: "Thou art my Son; this day have I begotten thee" (Psalms 2:7), "that God may be all in all" (I Corinthians 15:28). Then it can be said of us just as it was of Jesus: "And without controversy great is the mystery of godliness: God was manifest in the flesh, justified in the Spirit, seen of angels, preached unto the Gentiles, believed on in the world, received up into glory" (I Timothy 3:16). Though this was said of Jesus, it is eventually to be said of us, too.

> So also must my fall be healed. I cannot do the work without God, and God may not or will not without me; for if it shall be accomplished, in me, too, God must be made man; in such sort that God must take to himself all that is in me, within and without, so that there may be nothing in me which strives against God or hinders his Work.

There we have the complete picture. In each one of us "God must be made man." How? "God must take to himself all that is in me, within and without, so that there may be nothing in me which strives against God or hinders his Work." Often much of our work is simply in allowing the divine power to work in us the process of deification (*theosis*). For this is a work of restoration, not creation. We are being returned to the state we had originally and which Jesus re-entered before us, praying: "O Father, glorify thou me with thine own self with the glory which I had with thee before the world was" (John 17:5), "when the morning stars sang together, and all the sons of God shouted for joy" (Job 28:7).

> Now if God took to himself all men that are in the world, or ever were, and were made man in them, and they were made di-

vine in him, and this work were not fulfilled in me, my fall and my wandering would never be amended except it were fulfilled in me also.

Each person is destined for union with God, for godhood (Christhood). Yet since there is free will people can wander from life to life for creation cycles. Only in this sense is everlasting damnation possible; and it will be a self-sentence, a literal self-imprisonment.

And in this bringing back and healing, I can, or may, or shall do nothing of myself, but just simply yield to God, so that he alone may do all things in me and work, and I may allow him and all his work and his divine will.

That I have already pointed out.

And because I will not do so, but I count myself to be my own, and say "I," "Mine," "Me" and the like, God is hindered, so that he cannot do his work in me alone and without hindrance; for this cause my fall and my going astray remain unhealed. Behold! this all comes of my claiming somewhat for my own.

No comment needed. You cannot improve perfection.

The Perspective of Unity

(Chapter Four)

God says, "My glory will I not give to another" (Isaiah 42:8).
This is as much as to say, that praise and honor and glory be-
long to none but to God only. But now, if I call any good thing
my own, as if I were it, or of myself had power or did or knew
anything, or as if anything were mine or of me, or belonged to
me, or were due to me or the like, I take unto myself somewhat
of honor and glory, and do two evil things: First, I fall and go
astray as aforesaid: Secondly, I touch God in his honor and take
unto myself what belongs to God only. For all that must be
called good belongs to none but to the true eternal Goodness
which is God only, and whoso takes it unto himself, commits
unrighteousness and is against God.

All that we have and "are" is of God. Our very existence is drawn from
God. In the Bhagavad Gita God says: "I see the man of wisdom as my very
Self" (7:18). The enlightened see God as their inmost Self and God sees
them as part of his own Self. Distinction is there between God and man,
but no difference at all. This cannot be understood intellectually, but can
be experienced by the dedicated yogi.

We have nothing that did not come to us from God, therefore we can
claim nothing as ours, but rather all things we seem to have are really only
shared with us by God. When we say: "I am nothing, God is everything," we
are not denigrating ourselves but affirming that our life and value is God's
life and value. "My beloved is mine, and I am his" (Song of Solomon 2:16).

Although the experience of oneness with God is inexpressible by words,
Swami Sivananda made a valuable attempt in his poem, "Only God I Saw."

The final verses are:

> Like camphor I was melting in His fire of knowledge,
> Amidst the flames outflashing, only God I saw.
> My Prana entered the Brahmarandhra at the Moordha,
> Then I looked with God's eyes, only God I saw.
>
> I passed away into nothingness, I vanished,
> And lo, I was the all-living, only God I saw.
> I enjoyed the Divine Aisvarya, all God's Vibhutis,
> I had Visvaroopa Darshan, the Cosmic Consciousness,
> only God I saw.

Not Mine But Thine

(Chapter Five)

Certain men say that we ought to be without will, wisdom, love, desire, knowledge, and the like. Hereby is not to be understood that there is to be no knowledge in man, and that God is not to be loved by him, nor desired and longed for, nor praised and honored; for that were a great loss, and man were like the beasts and as the brutes that have no reason. But it means that man's knowledge should be so clear and perfect that he should acknowledge of a truth that in himself he neither has nor can do any good thing, and that none of his knowledge, wisdom and art, his will, love and good works do come from himself, nor are of man, nor of any creature, but that all these are of the eternal God, from whom they all proceed.

This has really been covered already. The necessity is to have the clear sight that all is of God without exception. "I live; yet not I, but Christ liveth in me" (Galatians 2:20). This realization was perfect (complete) in Jesus, and is to be so in every single human being. The greatest departure from Jesus' teachings was in making him unique, when he is the pattern for all. There is only one true religion: the path to union with God. And Yoga is the path.

As Christ himself says, "Without me ye can do nothing" (John 15:5). St. Paul says also, "What hast thou that thou didst not receive?" (I Corinthians 4:7). As much as to say: nothing. "Now if thou didst receive it, why dost thou glory, as if thou hadst not received it?" Again he says, "Not that we are sufficient

of ourselves to think any thing as of ourselves; but our sufficiency is of God" (II Corinthians 3:5).

Now when a man duly perceives these things in himself, he and the creature fall behind, and he does not call anything his own, and the less he takes this knowledge unto himself, the more perfect does it become. So also is it with the will, and love and desire, and the like. For the less we call these things our own, the more perfect and noble and Godlike do they become, and the more we think them our own, the baser and less pure and perfect do they become.

When this truth is realized then the individual lives in the consciousness Swami Sivananda expressed in "Only God I Saw." I witnessed for myself that Sivananda was a god upon earth, perfect in all things. He, too, was a Christ as was Jesus. And he truly saw all things as God. The more we see God the less do we see anything as separated from God. And ultimately we see only God.

Behold on this sort must we cast all things from us, and strip ourselves of them; we must refrain from claiming anything for our own. When we do this, we shall have the best, fullest, clearest and noblest knowledge that a man can have, and also the noblest and purest love, will and desire; for then these will be all of God alone. It is much better that they should be God's than the creature's.

This is a high ideal, but how can it be done? In one way only: filling the mind with the remembrance of God and occupying our mind only with things that are necessary. And even then, part of our mind must be holding on to the thought of God through constant repetition of a mantra. A mantra is a sound formula that transforms the consciousness. Repetition of a mantra is known as japa. More on this subject can be found in my books, *Soham Yoga, the Yoga of the Self.*

> Now that I ascribe anything good to myself, as if I were, or
> had done, or knew, or could perform any good thing, or that it
> were mine, this is all of sin and folly. For if the truth were rightly
> known by me, I should also know that I am not that good thing
> and that it is not mine, nor of me, and that I do not know it, and
> cannot do it, and the like. If this came to pass, I should needs
> cease to call anything my own.

If understood in the usual negative "Christian" way, this sounds like
extreme self-loathing and even self-nihilism. But it is not. It is an expression
of the consciousness that God is All in All. If we think we are creations then
we will consider ourselves nothing. But if we realize that we are totally part
of God, a wave of the divine sea of life, then we affirm our self-worth, for
God is our Self. Seeing ourselves as human is false and therefore deluding.
Seeing ourselves as god is true and freeing.

> It is better that God, or his works, should be known, as far
> as it be possible to us, and loved, praised and honored, and the
> like, and even that man should vainly imagine he loves or prais-
> es God, than that God should be altogether unpraised, unloved,
> unhonored and unknown.

Indifference, not hate, is the opposite of love. If something is hated
then it is thought about, and usually in a very personal way. So if God is
thought of, the very thought of God eventually opens the awareness of the
thinker and brings the thinker closer to him. The person who denounces,
argues and mocks God and religion is not far from the kingdom of God,
for he deliberately thinks of those things, which means that he has an inner
affinity for them and likes thinking about them. It is a matter of "just spell
my name right" in the long run.

I read an account of a Russian Orthodox Christian who was in a concentration camp for religious "offenders." He had noticed several Bibles
on a shelf in the main building. After becoming friends with one of the
guards who was sympathetic to the prisoners, he asked him to steal one

of the Bibles for him. "Oh, no," the guard told him, "If I did it would be noticed immediately, because every night the camp officials gather there and read them, sometimes for hours." And now the persecution is gone and many of the persecutors have been baptized. Truth alone prevails (*Satyam eva jayate*).

> For when the vain imagination and ignorance are turned into an understanding and knowledge of the truth, the claiming anything for our own will cease of itself. Then the man says: "Behold! I, poor fool that I was, imagined it was I, but behold! it is and was, of a truth, God!"

What a joyful revelation! And in time it will come to all: but only those who seek God inwardly and not outwardly, for as Jesus assures us: "The kingdom of God is within you." (Luke 17:21). "For the kingdom of God is… righteousness, and peace and joy in the Holy Ghost" (Romans 14:17).

Loved Above All

(Chapter Six)

A Master called Boetius says, "It is of sin that we do not love that which is Best." He has spoken the truth. That which is best should be the dearest of all things to us; and in our love of it, neither helpfulness nor unhelpfulness, advantage nor injury, gain nor loss, honor nor dishonor, praise nor blame, nor anything of the kind should be regarded; but what is in truth the noblest and best of all things, should be also the dearest of all things, and that for no other cause than that it is the noblest and best.

In a sketch of his remembrances of Saint German of Alaska (of the Russian Orthodox Church), Simeon Yanovsky writes, "Once the Elder was invited aboard a frigate which came from St. Petersburg. The captain of the frigate was a highly educated man, who had been sent to America by order of the Tsar to make an inspection of all the colonies. There were more than twenty-five officers with the captain, and they also were educated men. In the company of this group sat a monk of a hermitage, small in stature and wearing very old clothes. All these educated conversationalists were placed in such a position by his wise talks that they did not know how to answer him. The Captain himself used to say, 'We were lost for an answer before him.'

"Father German gave them all one general question: 'Gentlemen, What do you love above all, and what will each of you wish for your happiness?' Various answers were offered.... Some desired wealth, others glory, some a beautiful wife, and still others a beautiful ship he would captain; and so forth in the same vein. 'Is it not true,' Father Herman said to them concerning this, 'that all your various wishes can bring us to one conclusion—that each of you desires that which in his own understanding he considers the best, and which is most worthy of his love?' They all answered, 'Yes, that is so!' He then continued, 'Would you not say, Is not that which is best, above all, and surpassing all, and that which by preference is most worthy of love, the very Lord, who created us, adorned us with such ideals, gave life to all, sustains everything, nurtures and loves all, who is himself love and most beautiful of all? Should we not then love God above every thing, desire him more than anything, and search him out?'

"All said, 'Why, yes! That's self-evident!' Then the Elder asked, 'But do you love God?' They all answered, 'Certainly, we love God. How can we not love God?' 'And I have been trying for more than forty years to love God, I cannot say that I love Him completely,' Father German protested to them. He then began to demonstrate to them the way in which we should love God. 'If we love someone,' he said, 'we always remember them; we try to please them. Day and night our heart is concerned with the subject. Is that the way you gentlemen love God? Do you turn to Him often? Do you always remember Him? Do you always pray to Him and fulfill His holy commandments?' They had to admit that they had not! 'For our own good, and for our own fortune,' concluded the Elder, 'let us at least promise ourselves that from this very minute we will try to love God more than anything and to fulfill his holy will!' Without any doubt this conversation was imprinted in the hearts of the listeners for the rest of their lives."

> **Hereby may a man order his life within and without. His outward life: for among the creatures one is better than another, according as the Eternal Good manifests itself and works more in one than in another. Now that creature in which the Eternal Good most manifests itself, shines forth, works, is most known and loved, is the best, and that wherein the Eternal Good is least manifested is the least good of all creatures.**

There is a very important term in Indian philosophy: Swarupa. It literally means form (rupa) of the self (swa). A swarupa is the true appearance of something as well as its essence. It is a revelatory appearance. Seeing it, you see the thing itself as it truly is. In this section of *Theologia Germanica* we are told that the divine is manifested in different degrees in created things. The more the divine life is revealed in them, the more important and of value they are, and the wise love them as revealings of God who is indeed Good(ness).

In the Bhagavad Gita God himself tells us: "Whatever is glorious or prosperous or powerful, in every instance understand that it springs from but a fraction of my radiant Power" (Bhagavad Gita 10:41). Therefore those things are sought after by the wise and the true, whereas they pass by those things in which God is veiled rather than revealed. They consider that only the good is real and that which is not good is unreal. Insofar as they can, they act as though only the good exist and the rest do not exist.

> **Therefore when we have to do with the creatures and hold converse with them, and take note of their diverse qualities, the best creatures must always be the dearest to us, and we must cleave to them, and unite ourselves to them, above all to those which we attribute to God as belonging to him or divine, such as wisdom, truth, kindness, peace, love, justice, and the like. Hereby shall we order our outward man, and all that is contrary to these virtues we must eschew and flee from.**

In the Gita we are given this list of the divine powers (aishwarya) in man and the world: "I am... the knowledge of the Self; of debaters I am logic.... I am fame, prosperity, speech, memory, mental vigor, courage and endurance.... I am the splendor of the splendorous; I am victory and effort; I am the sattwa of the sattwic.... I am the power of rulers, I am the strategy of the ambitious, of secrets I am silence, the knowledge of knowers am I" (Bhagavad Gita 10:32, 34, 36, 38).

And further God tells us: "I am that which is the seed of all beings. There is nothing that could exist without existing through me" (Bhagavad Gita 10:39).

But if our inward man were to make a leap and spring into the Perfect, we should find and taste how that the Perfect is without measure, number or end, better and nobler than all which is imperfect and in part, and the Eternal above the temporal or perishable, and the fountain and source above all that flows or can ever flow from it. Thus that which is imperfect and in part would become tasteless and be as nothing to us. Be assured of this: All that we have said must come to pass if we are to love that which is noblest, highest and best.

If we are to truly "love that [God] which is noblest, highest and best" we must become one with him so his face is our face, his heart is our heart, his essence is our essence. "He leaves behind all the desires of the mind, contented in the Self by the Self" (Bhagavad Gita 2:55). "The yogi who is satisfied with knowledge and discrimination, unchanging, with senses conquered, to whom a lump of clay, a stone and gold are the same, steadfast—is said to be in union" (Bhagavad Gita 6:8). "He whose Self is unattached to external contacts, who finds happiness in the Self, whose Self is united to Brahman by yoga, reaches imperishable happiness" (Bhagavad Gita 5:21) "The yogi whose mind is truly tranquil, with emotions calmed, free of evil, having become one with Brahman, attains the supreme happiness. Thus constantly engaging himself in the practice of yoga, that yogi, freed from evil, easily touching Brahman, attains boundless happiness. He who is steadfast in yoga (yoga-yukta) at all times sees the Self present in all beings and all beings present in the Self. He who sees me everywhere, and sees all things in me—I am not lost to him, and he is not lost to me. He, established in unity, worships me dwelling in all things. Whatever be his mode of life, that yogi ever abides in me" (Bhagavad Gita 6:27-31).

THE CHRIST-SOUL

(CHAPTER SEVEN)

Losing the vision

It is a sad but true fact that the teachings of any master or world-teacher are misunderstood even during his life, and after his departure from this world there is a steady degeneration and distortion of his teachings until what remains is unrecognizable. It is rare that the teachings of a master survive even one generation unmarred. The many fundamental distortions of Jesus' teachings in the first three centuries formed the basis of a religion far from his original message.

The masters are always aware of the tenuous nature of their precepts. That is why Jesus, speaking of his future rebirth in this world, asked his disciples: "When the Son of man cometh, shall he find faith on the earth?" (Luke 18:8). "Many will say to me in that day, Lord, Lord, have we not prophesied in thy name? and in thy name have cast out devils? and in thy name done many wonderful works? And then will I profess unto them, I never knew you: depart from me, ye that work iniquity." (Matthew 7:22-23).

Many times Paramhansa Yogananda said to his disciples: "When I am gone you will all change everything." The first time I went into the bookstore at the Hollywood center in 1961, I met one of Yogananda's first New York City disciples, Annie Vickerman, the wife of Warren Vickerman, Yogananda's second American disciple. In our conversation she said: "Master more than once said to Vickie [her husband] and myself: 'After three generations you will not even know I came to this country.' When we asked him what use his coming here was, he told us: 'I have planted a seed and it will grow. My work will go on, even if my name is not mentioned.'"

In a letter to James Lynn (Rajasi Janakananda), who had asked about the future of the SRF organization after Yogananda's passing, Yoganandaji wrote, "I will go my way and they will go theirs."

He had no illusions about the future.

Confusion about Christ

One of the most harmful deviations from the original teachings of Jesus was the confusing of Jesus with Christ. "Christ" and "Christ Consciousness" are designations of Ishwara, the Lord, the personal creator aspect of God (Brahman). As an ordinary Christian I never met anyone who understood the doctrine of the Trinity or could speak a single intelligent sentence about it. But when I read the writings of Paramhansa Yogananda it was not just clear, it was simple. The Father is Brahman the transcendent absolute; the Son, the Only-Begotten, is Ishwara, the guiding consciousness within creation; the Holy Spirit is the Holy Breath, the intelligent Light from which all things are formed, Maha Shakti or Prakriti, the Mother aspect of God. The Trinity is not "three Persons" but three modes of the Divine in relation to the evolving consciousness that is the Self or Atman. God is absolutely one, but can manifest in a myriad ways. He is not confined by his unity to the simplistic monotheism of Western religions.

After all, Jesus was a missionary to the West, teaching the wisdom of the Eternal Religion (Sanatana Dharma) he had learned in India. There he had read: "But those great souls that abide in their divine nature, worship me single-mindedly, knowing me as the eternal Origin of beings. Always glorifying me and striving with firm vows, bowing to me with devotion, always steadfast, they worship me. And others, sacrificing by the sacrifice of knowledge, worship me as One and Manifold, variously manifested, omniscient" (Bhagavad Gita 9:13-15)

Although it is just a little over a century old, the most correct and complete presentation of the life and teachings of Jesus is *The Aquarian Gospel of Jesus the Christ* by Levi Dowling. There the right perspective on *the* Christ (Ishwara) and *a* Christ (a liberated master or avatar) is clearly shown.

"The news soon spread abroad that Jesus, king of Israel, had come to Bethany, and all the people of the town came forth to greet the king. And

Jesus, standing in the midst of them, exclaimed, Behold, indeed, the king has come, but Jesus is not king. The kingdom truly is at hand; but men can see it not with carnal eyes; they cannot see the king upon the throne. This is the kingdom of the soul; its throne is not an earthly throne; its king is not a man" (Aquarian Gospel 68:1-4).

"Men call me Christ, and God has recognized the name; but Christ is not a man. The Christ is universal love, and Love is king. This Jesus is but man who has been fitted by temptations overcome, by trials multiform, to be the temple through which Christ can manifest to men. Then hear, you men of Israel, hear! Look not upon the flesh; it is not king. Look to the Christ within, who shall be formed in every one of you, as he is formed in me. When you have purified your hearts by faith, the king will enter in, and you will see his face"(Aquarian Gospel 68:11-14).

Every sentient being is destined to become a Christ, and that is the subject of this chapter of *Theologia Germanica*.

> Let us remember how it is written and said that the soul of Christ had two eyes, a right and a left eye. In the beginning, when the soul of Christ was created, she fixed her right eye upon eternity and the Godhead, and remained in the full intuition and enjoyment of the divine Essence and Eternal Perfection; and continued thus unmoved and undisturbed by all the accidents and travail, suffering, torment and pain that ever befell the outward man. But with the left eye she beheld the creature and perceived all things therein, and took note of the difference between the creatures, which were better or worse, nobler or meaner; and thereafter was the outward man of Christ ordered.

We are all Christs by nature, but to manifest that nature requires the most exalted spiritual status. For us to attain that condition, God extended or emanated himself as Ishwara, the Son of God, the Christ. Here the priest is describing both this archetypal soul (psyche) and the soul of one who has attained Christhood: in this case the soul of Jesus.

The Christ-soul (Christ-psyche) has the ability to perceive the eternal and the temporal, the absolute and the relative, simultaneously and unceasingly. As the Bhagavad Gita says: "He who sees me everywhere, and sees all things in me–I am not lost to him, and he is not lost to me" (Bhagavad Gita 6:30). Such a one knows who and what he is: both divine and human. He lives in consciousness of his real being, and so is never distracted or unbalanced by the miseries of the world. "When the mind comes to rest, restrained by the practice of yoga, beholding the Self by the Self, he is content in the Self. He knows that endless joy which is apprehended by the buddhi beyond the senses; and established in that he does not deviate from the truth. Having attained this, he regards no other gain better than that, and established therein he is not moved by heaviest sorrow. Let this dissolution of union with pain be known as yoga. This yoga is to be practiced with determination, with an assured mind" (Bhagavad Gita 6:20-23).

The Christ-soul possesses the wisdom of viveka, of discrimination between the real and the unreal, the true and the false, and the real life it lives in God as well as the false life it lives in the world. There is no childlike naivité in such a one, but profound insight into the level and nature of everything they encounter in the relative world. The liberated not only know themselves, they know others equally well.

> **Thus the inner man of Christ, according to the right eye of his soul, stood in the full exercise of his divine nature, in perfect blessedness, joy and eternal peace. But the outward man and the left eye of Christ's soul, stood with him in perfect suffering, in all tribulation, affliction and travail; and this in such sort that the inward and right eye remained unmoved, unhindered and untouched by all the travail, suffering, grief and anguish that ever befell the outward man. It has been said that when Christ was bound to the pillar and scourged, and when he hung upon the cross, according to the outward man, yet his inner man, or soul according to the right eye, stood in as full possession of divine joy and blessedness as it did after his ascension, or as it does now. In like manner his outward man, or soul with the left eye,**

was never hindered, disturbed or troubled by the inward eye in
its contemplation of the outward things that belonged to it.

A Christ such as Krishna, Buddha and Jesus, lives in the state known
as Brahmanishtha or Brahmastithi–being established in the consciousness
of the Absolute Brahman, dwelling in that consciousness unbrokenly and
unwaveringly.

Now the created soul of man has also two eyes. The one is
the power of seeing into eternity, the other of seeing into time
and the creatures, of perceiving how they differ from each other
as afore-said, of giving life and needful things to the body, and
ordering and governing it for the best. But these two eyes of the
soul of man cannot both perform their work at once; but if the
soul shall see with the right eye into eternity, then the left eye
must close itself and refrain from working, and be as though it
were dead.

For if the left eye be fulfilling its office toward outward
things; that is, holding converse with time and the creatures;
then must the right eye be hindered in its working; that is, in its
contemplation. Therefore whosoever will have the one must let
the other go; for "no man can serve two masters."

The ordinary human soul which has not attained the status of a son of
God is either in the consciousness of the relative world (physical, astral or
causal) or in the realm of the spirit. The yogi lives in both to some degree,
but always one predominates. The experience of the spiritual world affects
him profoundly and results in his living the life of the world with the
spiritual perspective that transforms his mode of life in the world and his
reaction to it. More and more "this corruptible must put on incorruption,
and this mortal must put on immortality. So when this corruptible shall
have put on incorruption, and this mortal shall have put on immortality,
then shall be brought to pass the saying that is written, Death is swallowed
up in victory" (I Corinthians 15:53-54).

For the yogi, life increases day by day as death fades away day by day until only the divine life remains, and he is free. Then the two "eyes" have become one, seeing as God sees, not as man sees. Then his eye is "single" as we have seen earlier in this study. Living the state of unity he sees only unity, but a unity that embraces the dualities in the relative planes of life. Since the world comes from God, embodies the will of God and is evolving back to God, eventually the "left eye" merges into the "right eye" and the "masters" that seemed dual and antithetical earlier are seen to be but the One. Then the Christ-soul has become god, has become a perfect reflection-image of the Father, the Son and the Holy Spirit, Trinity in Unity and Unity in Trinity.

Making the Impossible Possible

(Chapter Eight)

It has been asked whether it be possible for the soul, while it is yet in the body, to reach so high as to cast a glance into eternity, and receive a foretaste of eternal life and eternal blessedness. This is commonly denied; and truly so in a sense. For it indeed cannot be so long as the soul is taking heed to the body, and the things which minister and appertain thereto, and to time and the creature, and is disturbed and troubled and distracted thereby.

It has always amazed me that Western Christianity stubbornly clings to the idea that no one living in a physical body can see or know God. The Western Church has persecuted and executed quite a number of people who claimed they could see or had seen God. The Eastern Church, on the other hand, believes that it is possible for anyone to see God if it is the divine will. It teaches that when Jesus was transfigured the light which shone from him and seen by the apostles was the Uncreated Light of God.

Richard Rolle of Hampole (England) who was a contemporary of the Teutonic Priest also taught the same. Rolle had the good sense to quit studying for the priesthood when he came to the point in his studies where he was expected to debate theological concepts in class, sometimes speaking for an idea and then against it. This kind of literal sophistry disgusted him so he became a hermit. He never argued about the matter of seeing uncreated light, but just mentioned it casually in his writings as a fact.

The Frankfurter, however, is tackling the idea even though it could have gotten him in grave trouble and maybe been burnt for heresy. Because of this he attempts to soothe potential heresy-hunters by saying that being unable to see and experience God is "truly so in a sense" and then shows that anyone can see God who strives to ascend in consciousness.

Those who identify with the body and the world around it cannot see God—not because they are evil or God refuses to be seen by worldly people, but because they lack the requisite level of evolution, which includes extreme subtlety of perception. The more the aspirant works to experience the highest levels within his own being, the more he becomes able to see the unseeable. Jesus was referring to this when he said: "Lay up for yourselves treasures in heaven,… For where your treasure is, there will your heart be also" (Matthew 6:20-21). By "heart" he means the inmost core or being, the pure consciousness that is our spirit. And "heaven" is the rarefied "space of consciousness" (chidakasha) where the heart must be habituated to ascend and dwell. He continued the idea by saying further: "The light of the body is the eye: if therefore thine eye be single, thy whole body shall be full of light" (Matthew 6:22). By "eye" he means the center of our consciousness. To *see* spirit we must first *be* spirit.

There is the world and there is heaven—material consciousness and divine spiritual consciousness. "No man can serve two masters: for either he will hate the one, and love the other; or else he will hold to the one, and despise the other. Ye cannot serve God and mammon" (Matthew 6:24). This is extremely crucial to understand. It is a matter of polarity on all levels. The world is negative in polarity (not evil or sinful) and our essential being (and God) is positive in polarity, ultimately canceling each other out. So we must decide where we will direct our life current and consciousness.

I met a man who had three families. Illegal as it was, he had married three women. He divided his time between the families and at the same time kept insisting to a friend of mine that they should be "close." "I won't marry you, honey," he told her, "but I will show you how to live!" Being a serious yogi she declined the offer. But many people would like to make such an arrangement with God, which by its nature is impossible to manage.

> For if the soul shall rise to such a state, she must be quite pure, wholly stripped and bare of all images, and be entirely separate from all creatures, and above all from herself.

There is no way to attain this state of purification except through meditation, and by that I mean yoga practice. Mere willing and wishing accomplish nothing. The exact methodology of yoga is necessary.

> Now many think this is not to be done and is impossible in this present time. But St. Dionysius maintains that it is possible, as we find from his words in his Epistle to Timothy, where he says: "For the beholding of the hidden things of God, shalt you forsake sense and the things of the flesh, and all that the senses can apprehend, and all that reason of her own powers can bring forth, and all things created and uncreated that reason is able to comprehend and know, and shalt take your stand upon an utter abandonment of yourself, and as knowing none of the aforesaid things, and enter into union with him who is, and who is above all existence and all knowledge." Now if he did not hold this to be possible in this present time, why should he teach it and enjoin it on us in this present time?

How shocked the Frankfurter would have been if he had been told that a few centuries after his citing Saint Dionysius the Areopagite the Western Church would brand Saint Dionysius' writings as unauthentic–not his work at all but an imposture. For the Eastern Christians, however, Saint Dionysius is still the supreme authority on mysticism. So we may analyze his words in complete confidence.

For the beholding of the hidden things of God, shalt you forsake sense and the things of the flesh, and all that the senses can apprehend. Saint Dionysius means this literally. To see the depths of God we must go beyond the senses and the body and all things that can be perceived by the senses. In other words, we must become immaterial, as is God, to see the things of

God and God himself. While in the body we must become totally spirit as well. Again, yoga is the means to achieve this.

And all that reason of her own powers can bring forth, and all things created and uncreated that reason is able to comprehend and know. Not just the sensory mind, but the intellect (buddhi) must be gone beyond. In meditation thoughts, memories, impressions and concepts must be banished from the focus of the yogi's attention.

And shalt take your stand upon an utter abandonment of yourself, and as knowing none of the aforesaid things. When the seeker casts aside all egoic feeling and conditioning as well as any "knowing," then he will stand forth as his true Self and will see and know God. Then he, too, can say with Jesus: "I and My Father are one" (John 10:30).

And enter into union with him who is, and who is above all existence and all knowledge. "And God said unto Moses, I AM THAT I AM" (Exodus 3:14). God does not exist in the way that we know as existence, which is a momentary and relative appearance and existence. God is absolute Being: AM. And so are we. So knowledge of our Self is impossible without knowledge of God. God cannot be known as an object, but as eternal subject. All are known by him, but none know him through their finite mind. "Veiled by Yogamaya, I am not manifest to all. This deluded world perceives me not who am unborn and imperishable. I know the departed beings and the living, and those who are yet to be, but none whatsoever knows me" (Bhagavad Gita 7:25-26).

Yet when they divest themselves of all that is finite and relative and "put on Christ" (Galatians 3:27), the nature that they possess in common with God, then they will live in that status even here in this world.

But it behoves you to know that a master has said on this passage of St. Dionysius, that it [perfect knowing of God while in the flesh] is possible, and may happen to a man often, till he become so accustomed to it, as to be able to look into eternity whenever he will. For when a thing is at first very hard to a man and strange, and seemingly quite impossible, if he put all his strength and energy into it, and persevere therein, that will

afterward grow quite light and easy, which he at first thought quite out of reach, seeing that it is of no use to begin any work, unless it may be brought to a good end.

It would be interesting to know who the "master" was that agreed with Saint Dionysius, since he, like the Frankfurter, would be out of step with the common theology of the day. Nevertheless, what is said is true: the yogi can become so accustomed to reaching the heights of meditation that he can do so as often as he wishes, since he first did so through a methodology whose repetition will produce the same results whenever he does it. There is nothing haphazard here. I will never forget how relieved I was when I learned of yoga and realized there was no longer any need to cover up lack or failure by blaming it on whether God "willed" my success or not; that God had done all the needful. From there on it was all up to me. Fake religion has to invent various means to gloss over its inadequacies, but such charlatanry has no place in yoga. Not only is yoga the only true religion, it is also the only true science. Yoga never fails, ensuring that the yogi and his attempts will without doubt "be brought to a good end."

And a single one of these excellent glances is better, worthier, higher and more pleasing to God, than all that the creature can perform as a creature.

Here we have it! The thing that made the theologians of his day so insistent that God could not be seen and experienced, that to attempt it was delusional and of course heretical: the plain truth that a single mystical experience eclipses all the external trappings and good deeds of exoteric religion, and life dedicated to such a pursuit is as far from their life as heaven from earth. Saint Thomas Aquinas wrote many volumes which became the basis of much Catholic theology. At the end of his life he had a profound mystical experience (during which he levitated). Later when his assistant asked him to continue dictating an unfinished theological work, he said: "I cannot, because all that I have written seems like straw to me." This incident unsettles those who cling to exoteric theology devoid of mysticism.

Absence of evil is not the same as good. Good is a living, dynamic power, and since God alone is good (Matthew 19:17), only the quest for God-realization is the good life. All else is truly a shameful waste. It does not matter to such self-committed slaves that Jesus said the contemplative way of Mary was not only the best, but that she would never lose its blessings, whereas Martha had chosen nothing but business and worry and the egoic obsession with "service." (See Luke 10:38-42). "We need Marthas as much as Marys!" they petulantly insist, seeking to hide the truth of themselves and their shallow lives and tokens of religion.

Later on Mary dared to pour expensive perfume on Jesus's head. Judas and all those like him were/are indignant at the "waste" devoted souls engage in when they give their all to God and not to man (Mark 14:3-9), especially those that "hide themselves away" in a monastery or convent. Of this be assured: No one needs Judases as much as Johns. Of course the world sees it differently, even though Saint James, the brother of John, says to us: "Know ye not that the friendship of the world is enmity with God? whosoever therefore will be a friend of the world is the enemy of God" (James 4:4). "Fanatical," isn't it? Just like Jesus who chose the cross rather than the "Good Life." He just had to stand out from the crowd, didn't he? And set the example for those coming after who "loved not their lives unto the death" (Revelation 12:11).

And as soon as a man turns himself in spirit, and with his whole heart and mind enters into the mind of God which is above time, all that ever he has lost is restored in a moment.

Those who truly turn to God wholeheartedly will have the mind of Christ (I Corinthians 2:16). They will see as God sees, and value as God values. They will possess the kingdom of God, which is the mind of God; and all seeming sacrifice will be seen as nothing. And whatever has truly been sacrificed will be returned to them in their higher, spiritual forms.

And if a man were to do thus a thousand times in a day, each time a fresh and real union would take place; and in this sweet

and divine work stands the truest and fullest union that may be in this present time.

Who would give their life to pursue "this sweet and divine work"? Only the wise. The others will follow this scenario: "A certain man made a great supper, and bade many: And sent his servant at supper time to say to them that were bidden, Come; for all things are now ready. And they all with one consent began to make excuse. The first said unto him, I have bought a piece of ground, and I must needs go and see it: I pray thee have me excused. And another said, I have bought five yoke of oxen, and I go to prove them: I pray thee have me excused. And another said, I have married a wife, and therefore I cannot come" (Luke 14:16-20).

For he who has attained thereto, asks nothing further, for he has found the Kingdom of Heaven and Eternal Life on earth.

The wise will seek it and the foolish will wait. The wise will pay the price and the foolish will wait for the price to be reduced. Which will never happen.

The Inner Versus the Outer; God Versus the World

(Chapter Nine)

We should mark and know of a very truth that all manner of virtue and goodness, and even that Eternal Good which is God himself, can never make a man virtuous, good, or happy, so long as it is outside the soul; that is, so long as the man is holding converse with outward things through his senses and reason, and does not withdraw into himself and learn to understand his own life, who and what he is.

I once read a satirical story in which a completely foolish woman decided to commit suicide. So one night she put a knife under her pillow, but in the morning was still alive. The next night she got more drastic and put some bullets under her pillow. But in the morning she somehow was still alive. The next night she put some poison under her pillow, but with the same non-result. It is the same in spiritual life. If virtue and goodness, the effects of spiritual wisdom, do not get inside us, they have no effect on us and we are wasting our time.

To put it plainly, God and religion are meaningless to those who do not cultivate the interior life and make their inner being their continual abode. For it is a prime necessity that every person "withdraw into himself and learn to understand his own life, who and what he is." Otherwise his life is meaningless and useless. Belief in God, praising God, obeying God and even giving up our life for God are worthless if we do not find God

47

within us and become one with God in the fullest sense. This has nothing to do with the childish "let Jesus come into your heart" of fundamentalist Protestantism. It is a state of consciousness and being, not a snuggey lovey warmey feeling somewhere inside.

> **The like is true of sin and evil. For all manner of sin and wickedness can never make us evil, so long as it is outside of us; that is, so long as we do not commit it, or do not give consent to it.**

Evil is twofold: external and internal. If we refrain from these forms, then evil cannot contaminate us. This being so, we should realize that if we do not think about or react to them in any way, we will be guiltless and at peace. The wise do not engage in the pointless exercise of talking about the evil of others and being indignant about external conditions over which they have no control or influence. If there is nothing we can do about external evil we should ignore it, shielding ourselves from it if we are somehow threatened by it. This does not mean that we accept evil or become callous to it, but that we do not touch it either outwardly or inwardly.

> **Therefore although it be good and profitable that we should ask, and learn and know, what good and holy men have wrought and suffered, and how God has dealt with them, and what he has wrought in and through them, yet it were a thousand times better that we should in ourselves learn and perceive and understand, who we are, how and what our own life is, what God is and is doing in us, what he will have from us, and to what ends he will or will not make use of us.**

Admiring saints and great masters is good if that inspires us to follow their examples. But just admiring or even worshipping holy men and women, even if they are avatars, means nothing if we do not determine to ourselves become like them. Belief in and praise of the holy will lead us to nothing if we do not strive to be holy ourselves. Those who truly believe in God and his saints strive to become one with God and be numbered with his saints in the highest worlds. We must take seriously and apply to ourselves the statement of Jesus: "He that believeth on me, the works that I do shall he do also; and greater works than these shall he do" (John 14:12). He makes no exceptions.

> **For, of a truth, thoroughly to know oneself, is above all art, for it is the highest art. If you know yourself well, you are better and more praiseworthy before God, than if you did not know yourself, but did understand the course of the heavens and of all the planets and stars, also the dispositions of all mankind, also the nature of all beasts, and, in such matters, hadst all the skill of all who are in heaven and on earth. For it is said, there came a voice from heaven, saying, "Man, know yourself." Thus that proverb is still true, "Going out were never so good, but staying at home were much better."**

This is extremely clear. But why should we know our Self? Because God is at the core of our Self, and therefore the way to know God is to first know our Self.

It is of course wonderful that a Christian (and a priest at that) should have the insights found in this book. And it is equally wondrous that he cites the aphorism "Man, know yourself," which was one of the maxims inscribed in the forecourt of the Temple of Apollo at Delphi. This indicates that he believed the oracle was not a mouthpiece of demons, as "orthodox" Christianity claims today, but an oracle giving divine wisdom, and therefore of God. And since *Theologia Germanica* has been read and valued for centuries by Christian (especially Catholic) mystics, it obviously expresses what is the true orthodoxy of Christ's teachings. In many instances people have to quit being church members if they would truly follow Christ. This is not so surprising when we consider that Saint Paul's words: "Ye are the body of Christ, and members in particular" (I Corinthians 12:27), were directed to *people*, to individual believers, and not to an organization.

People are very skilled in making substitutes for God; and "the Church," like the Bible and doctrine, is one of them.

The second citation also goes against popular "workaday" Christianity which is absorbed in externals of every kind. Going on missions and "working/witnessing for Jesus" are favorite expressions of this attitude. But since the Self, the spirit, is the focus of the priest-knight, he recommends staying home and minding our own business: which is aspiring and working toward the knowledge of our Self and of God, total union with God in which the enlightened one knows himself as god within God, inseparable and eternal. Obviously our author is a forerunner of the hated and persecuted Quietists of the seventeenth century, whose writings are invaluable.

> **Further, you should learn that eternal blessedness lies in one thing alone, and in nought else. And if ever man or the soul is to be made blessed, that one thing alone must be in the soul. Now some might ask, "But what is that one thing?" I answer, it is Goodness, or that which has been made good; and yet neither this good nor that, which we can name, or perceive or show; but it is all and above all good things.**

God is the true good. "Behold, one came and said unto him, Good Master, what good thing shall I do, that I may have eternal life? And he said unto him, Why callest thou me good? there is none good but one, that is, God" (Matthew 19:16-17), and that which God has assumed into himself and made good by making it god. None of the things of earth can go through this alchemy; nothing of "this" or "that," but only the spirit-souls of sentient beings.

> **Moreover, it needs not to enter into the soul, for it is there already, only it is unperceived. When we say we should come unto it, we mean that we should seek it, feel it, and taste it.**

God is always seated at the center of our spirit; each one of us is a throne of God, even if we do not realize or even deny it. "I am the

Self abiding in the heart of all beings; I am the beginning, the middle and the end of all beings as well" (Bhagavad Gita 10:20). "The Lord dwells in the hearts of all beings" (Bhagavad Gita 18:61). "But those in whom this ignorance of the Self has been destroyed by knowledge–that knowledge of theirs, like the sun, reveals the Supreme Brahman. Those whose minds are absorbed in That, whose Selves are fixed on That, whose foundation is That, who hold That as the highest object, whose evils have been shaken off by knowledge, attain the ending of rebirth" (Bhagavad Gita 5:16-17).

Although God is within each one of us, we must seek him, feel him and taste him. "O taste and see that the Lord is good" (Psalms 34:8). "Commune with your own heart, and be still" (Psalms 4:4). "Be still, and know that I am God" (Psalms 46:10).

> **And now since it is One, unity and singleness is better than manifoldness. For blessedness lies not in much and many, but in One and oneness. In one word, blessedness lies not in any creature, or work of the creatures, but it lies alone in God and in his works.**

Non-dual consciousness is the consciousness of God and those who, having become one with him, are "his works." The blessed live in union with the Blesser. We should never be satisfied with the consciousness of the many, but make ourselves one in all things: seeing and being only the One. Unity is the only truth, the only good, the only God.

> **Therefore I must wait only on God and his work, and leave on one side all creatures with their works, and first of all myself.**

The first step toward God is leaving our ego behind and merging our consciousness in God. Yet people assume that is the last step, not realizing that the real Life in Christ only begins where most people think spiritual life ends, or declare that such a step is impossible or unreasonable. Only those who leave all things behind will find themselves and thereby come to possess all things as God possesses them. As Yogananda wrote in a simple chant:

> I will lose myself in my Self,
> in Savikalpa Samadhi Yoga.
> I will find myself in my Self,
> in Nirvikalpa Samadhi Yoga.

Savikalpa samadhi is the samadhi (superconscious state) in which there is objective experience or experience of "qualities" and with the triad of knower, knowledge and known. It is meditation with limited external awareness. Nirvikalpa samadhi is the samadhi in which there is no objective experience or experience of "qualities" whatsoever, and in which the triad of knower, knowledge and known does not exist. It is purely subjective experience of the formless, qualityless and unconditioned Absolute, the highest state of samadhi, beyond all thought, attribute and description.

> **In like manner all the great works and wonders that God has ever wrought or shall ever work in or through the creatures, or even God himself with all his goodness, so far as these things exist or are done outside of me, can never make me blessed, but only in so far as they exist and are done and loved, known, tasted and felt within me.**

"Behold, the kingdom of God is within you" (Luke 17:21). Therefore God is within us and the search for the kingdom and the King is an inner search.

"Great is that yogi who seeks to be [one] with Brahman, greater than those who mortify the body, greater than the learned, greater than the doers of good works: therefore, become a yogi" (Bhagavad Gita 6:46).

WISDOM AND FOLLY

(CHAPTER TEN)

> Now let us mark: Where men are enlightened with the true
> light, they perceive that all which they might desire or choose,
> is nothing to that which all creatures, as creatures, ever desired
> or chose or knew. Therefore they renounce all desire and choice,
> and commit and commend themselves and all things to the
> Eternal Goodness.

One of the best ways to learn is to observe others and avoid making
their mistakes. So the Frankfurter is telling us that if we look at the entire
human race yearning and struggling to get everything under the sun we
will see that they usually do not get what they want, or if they do they
eventually lose it, or having gotten it they either lose interest in it or find
it makes them more unhappy than they were before they got it. Swami
Brahmananda, the disciple of Sri Ramakrishna, said: "If you give your
mind and heart to the world it will destroy them," for that is the way of
the world.

We must save ourselves from such destruction by turning to God
instead, desiring and seeking union with him alone. The Lord Jesus said:
"Seek ye first the kingdom of God, and his righteousness; and all these
things shall be added unto you" (Matthew 6:33) if they are good, or the
desire for them will fade away and you will be free. In many instances when
we are not intelligent or mentally strong enough to turn from the things
of the world, karma steps in and makes it impossible for us to have them.
We should not only be thankful when God answers our petitions, but also
when he does not. If we put God first at all times, we will be protected
from great suffering and disillusionment.

> Nevertheless, there remains in them a desire to go forward and get nearer to the Eternal Goodness; that is, to come to a clearer knowledge, and warmer love, and more comfortable assurance, and perfect obedience and subjection; so that every enlightened man could say: "I would fain be to the Eternal Goodness, what his own hand is to a man."

Those who cease wanting the things of this world and become indifferent to them, and to the world itself, while at the same time desiring God with their whole heart, will not become apathetic or wander through life like zombies, but rather will experience the assurance of God through the prophet Jeremiah: "Ye shall seek me, and find me, when ye shall search for me with all your heart" (Jeremiah 29:13). And to Abraham: "I am thy shield, and thy exceeding great reward" (Genesis 15:1). Just think: God has promised himself to us–not the perishable things of this or any world. Then we, too, can say: "My beloved is mine, and I am his" (Song of Solomon 2:16). We should heed the following parable of Sri Ramakrishna:

"Once upon a time a wood-cutter went into a forest to chop wood. There suddenly he met a brahmachari. The holy man said to him, 'My good man, go forward.' On returning home the wood-cutter asked himself, 'Why did the brahmachari tell me to go forward?' Some time passed. One day he remembered the brahmachari's words. He said to himself, 'Today I shall go deeper into the forest.' Going deep into the forest, he discovered innumerable sandal-wood trees. He was very happy and returned with cart-loads of sandal-wood. He sold them in the market and became very rich.

"A few days later he again remembered the words of the holy man to go forward. He went deeper into the forest and discovered a silver-mine near a river. This was even beyond his dreams. He dug out silver from the mine and sold it in the market. He got so much money that he didn't even know how much he had.

"A few more days passed. One day he thought: 'The brahmachari didn't ask me to stop at the silver-mine; he told me to go forward.' This time he went to the other side of the river and found a gold-mine. Then he exclaimed: 'Ah, just see! This is why he asked me to go forward.'

"Again, a few days afterwards, he went still deeper into the forest and found heaps of diamonds and other precious gems. He took these also and became as rich as the god of wealth himself.

"Therefore I say that, whatever you may do, you will find better and better things if only you go forward.... If you go still farther you will realize God. You will see Him. In time you will converse with Him."

I would fain be to the Eternal Goodness, what his own hand is to a man. What are our hands to us? They are a part of our body and accomplish that which we will to do. They are a part of "us." So those who say the foregoing sentence aspire to be a part of God, instruments of his will and work, to be god and live and act as god. Saint Teresa of Avila wrote: "Christ has no body now on earth but yours; no hands but yours; no feet but yours; yours are the eyes through which Christ's compassion is to look out to the earth; yours are the feet by which he is to go about doing good; and yours are the hands by which he is to bless us now." Jesus was a hand of the Father, and we can be the same.

> **And he fears always that he is not enough so, and longs for the salvation of all men.**

There is no self-satisfaction or self-congratulation in the heart of the true lover and servant of God. There, too, he seeks to ever go forward until the distinction of "he and I" disappears from his consciousness.

In the second half of this sentence the author indicates the ultimate salvation of all human beings, for it would not be wisdom to long for that which is impossible. Obviously our priest-knight believes that eventually God shall "be all in all" (I Corinthians 15:28). Everlasting damnation is impossible, and everlasting salvation alone is possible. This is the perfection of God's purpose in manifesting the creation and sending us forth within it. "For the earnest expectation of the creature waiteth for the manifestation of the sons of God" (Romans 8:19).

> **And such men do not call this longing their own, nor take it unto themselves, for they know well that this desire is not of**

man, but of the Eternal Goodness; for whatsoever is good shall no one take unto himself as his own, seeing that it belongs to the Eternal Goodness, only.

The aspiration for perfection within God, as a god, is the direct action of God. Therefore those who have such an aspiration in truth (many talk it but do not intend to attain it) are already manifesting their god-nature. In them God is acting as their inmost being and enlightening their minds and hearts.

One of my cousins was what in former days was delicately known as "a naughty girl," yet my Aunt Faye (not her mother) and I loved her and were her only true family. She could always count on us to love and welcome her. Unhappily her wayward ways ultimately brought about her death in an automobile accident. Aunt Faye was deeply grieved because her religion taught that Margaret would be consigned to hell forever. "Do you really believe that we love Margaret more than God does?" I asked her. "Neither you nor I would send her to hell, so why do you think God will? We understood Margaret's failings, so how could an omniscient God not understand as well? We always looked at her with love–will God do less?" But ignorant religion won out and Aunt Faye carried in her heart the burden of thinking Margaret was damned forever by a God of love whom the Bible says *is* love. God is not in such a religion, and God is not acting in those who cling to it. But since all shall be made perfect in God eventually, we need not argue or blame but rejoice and give thanks to God that salvation is the destiny of all without exception.

Moreover, these men are in a state of freedom, because they have lost the fear of pain or hell, and the hope of reward or heaven, but are living in pure submission to the Eternal Goodness, in the perfect freedom of fervent love.

Not desiring heaven and not fearing hell is the freedom of those in whom the divine leaven has begun to work. It is the sign that all-encompassing love for both God and man has arisen and is increasing in them as they progress toward the perfection of the divine image within them. God has begun to live and love in them.

This mind was in Christ in perfection, and is also in his followers, in some more, and in some less.

The disciples of Christ must of necessity "put on Christ" (Galatians 3:27), for "to them gave he power to become the sons of God" (John 1:12), for to them "God would make known the glory of this mystery; which is Christ in you, the hope of glory" (Colossians 1:27), in order that they may truthfully say without vanity or boasting: "We have the mind of Christ" (I Corinthians 2:16), and therefore desire what Christ desired and attain what Christ attained. Now there may be differing degrees of the mind of Christ in different seekers, but in time there will be complete equality of vision so finally they shall "all come in the unity of the faith, and of the knowledge of the Son of God, unto a perfect man, unto the measure of the stature of the fulness of Christ" (Ephesians 4:13).

But it is a sorrow and shame to think that the Eternal Goodness is ever most graciously guiding and drawing us, and we will not yield to it.

This is a great tragedy, but true. "Man's inhumanity to God" is a very real factor in the miseries of the world. Yogananda said: "In one of His aspects, a very touching aspect, the Lord may be said to be a beggar. He yearns for our attention. The Master of the Universe, at whose glance all stars, moons, and planets quiver, is running after man and saying: 'Won't you give me your love? Won't you seek me? Don't you love me, the Giver, more than the things I have made for you?' But man says: 'I am too busy now; I have work to do. I can't take time to look for You.' And the Lord says: 'I will wait.'"

God has done all that is needed for us to seek and find him and end ignorance and suffering forever; but most people not only do not believe it, they actively deny it and mock those who do believe. Speaking through

Isaiah, God has said: "I have spread out my hands all the day unto a rebellious people, which walketh in a way that was not good, after their own thoughts" (Isaiah 65:2). And Saint Paul says that God says: "All day long I have stretched forth my hands unto a disobedient and gainsaying people" (Romans 10:21). The vast majority of humanity ignore, deny and defy God. Yet, as Yogananda said, God will wait. Such is his love for all. And eventually they shall hear the call and seek and find God.

What is better and nobler than true poorness in spirit?

"Blessed are the poor in spirit [*ptochoi to pneumati*]" (Matthew 5:3). Kenneth Wuest in his *The New Testament, An Expanded Translation* renders this: "the destitute and helpless in the realm of the spirit." Now that does not sound very blessed, however the qualifying words "of the spirit" can help us understand. This beatitude is speaking of an attitude, of a practical view which we should hold regarding ourselves. But this attitude will in its fruition also be the impetus for spiritual activity. To be destitute and helpless is to both possess nothing and to be unable to do anything. Before we reject this as a negative and unworthy ideal, we must realize that we are dealing with the world of the Absolute in which what is undesirable in the world of relative existence is often an expression of the highest good.

We must distinguish between nothing and No Thing. The failure to grasp this distinction has caused many to misunderstand the teaching of Buddhism regarding The Great Void, which is not pure Absence as many think, but is in actuality pure Presence, the totality of being. Nothing and No Thing are literally poles apart, for "nothing" is just that: nothing, zero. But No Thing is the Source of All and is in essence Everything.

Here in the world of relativity we are dragged along by things. Whether they be our minds, emotions, attachments, possessions, bodily needs, or the demands of others, whatever motivates us or stimulates us to keep on racing in the hamster wheel of conditioned existence is external to us: a *thing*. In the domain of spirit, to be destitute is actually to be divested of all things, to be self-existent and therefore self-sufficient, to rest in our true essence which, being potentially infinite, is also potentially all-encompassing. It is the Emptiness that is perfect Fulness. But that Fulness is unattainable as long as we possess, or are possessed by, a single mote. Therefore, those who are totally divested of all things whatsoever are truly blessed, for they may come to possess The All.

To be helpless in the highest sense is to be in a state beyond all doing whatsoever. Divinity in Its pure essence is transcendent, utterly beyond all motion and change, the Eternal Witness. Within itself it contains all the individualized consciousnesses for whose sake it has expanded or emanated Itself as all the spheres of relative existence. As long as those consciousnesses are involved in the evolutionary currents of those innumerable worlds, they experience change, which is contradictory to their essential nature which is unchanging. Their very presence in those worlds is a fundamental self-denial, just as it is for the Deity, who for that reason is pictured as the cosmic man crucified upon the cross of matter. The crucifix is not just a depiction of the death of Jesus of Nazareth. It is a portrayal of both man and cosmos.

In order to do anything, the consciousness must be both within a region of relativity and in possession of some faculty or adjunct alien to its nature by which it can act upon its environment. God and the individual spirit being beyond all relativity and in need of nothing, obviously do nothing. Since action is antithetical to its very nature, then a spirit that is perfectly and irrevocably established in its true being is incapable of doing anything.

God and the perfect spirit are, then, destitute and helpless in the blessed state known as being poor in spirit. For theirs alone is the Kingdom of Heaven. Having no thing, they both have and are one with the All. To possess infinity! Those who truly grasp the inner meaning of this first beatitude gladly set about divesting themselves of "things" and begin the blessed process of unlearning so they may at last attain to gnosis. Their lives must be increasingly simplified to reveal the essence of living. In their inner silence they come to be knowers of the Word. And all this they do through meditation and a spirit-oriented life.

Yet when that is held up before us, we will have none of it, but are always seeking ourselves, and our own things.

Immersed in delusion we do not realize that we already have and are our true Self, that the elusive things we seek after are mirages. Furthermore, nothing can ever be ours, because the possessive ego can own nothing. This is why greedy people frantically spend their lives accumulating more and more. They cannot be satisfied, for the ego cannot be satisfied: it is an illusion seeking more illusion. On the other hand those who know their Self which lives in God possess all things, for all things are not just owned by God, they *are* God the Holy Spirit, the creative Power which manifests as all things. There are no things, ever; there is only God. As Emily Bronte wrote:

> Though earth and moon were gone
> And suns and universes ceased to be
> And Thou wert left alone
> Every Existence would exist in thee.

We like to have our mouths always filled with good things, that we may have in ourselves a lively taste of pleasure and sweetness. When this is so, we are well pleased, and think it stands not amiss with us. But we are yet a long way off from a perfect life.

For this reason we cannot be completely happy or satisfied, and much of our life is spent in covering this fact up–deluding ourselves. Before we can know our true Self we have to understand the nature of our false self and its false world. Death takes from us all that we have and seem to be, but dying while addicted to things brings us back to this world where we again spend a lifetime grabbing at that which is essentially non-existent. As Wordsworth wrote: "Getting and spending, we lay waste our powers." We lose everything in the attempt to satisfy by material and psychological means that which is purely spirit: our own Self.

For when God will draw us up to something higher, that is, to an utter loss and forsaking of our own things, spiritual and

natural, and withdraws his comfort and sweetness from us, we faint and are troubled, and can in no wise bring our minds to it; and we forget God and neglect holy exercises, and fancy we are lost for ever.

This is an extremely important subject. A child grows up and the things and toys that he used to like and spend hours with seem silly and boring to him. He does not have to exert will power to abandon them, his mental growth brings it about automatically. In the same way when someone progresses spiritually his perspective and relationship with the world and the things in it will change. What used to satisfy no longer does so, but seems flat and stale or even distasteful. What attracted him may now even repulse him. Since most people are addicted to "happiness" and "satisfaction," when this occurs they go into a veritable tailspin. If they continue in that limbo then they experience utter misery and call it "the dark night of the soul," when it really is the result of refusing to grow up spiritually. Only by drastic change on the physical, mental and spiritual levels can any emerge into the light of higher awareness.

It is true that many people think that they are abandoned by God or that life itself has become meaningless and dreary. Since they are used to indulging themselves with passing moods and fancies, they continue to do so and sink into the swamp of dullness and despair. Often this is the end of their spiritual life for that incarnation.

When a child grows and his shoes no longer fit he realizes it and tells his parents so new shoes can be gotten. But unhappily almost no one has this understanding of the spiritual situation and knows what to do about it. Just as the parent birds get their young to stand on the edge of the nest and then push them off so they will fly, in the same way God (and our higher self) is dealing with us. You cannot go to a new and better place without leaving the old and unsatisfactory place behind. In spiritual life, too, you cannot have the cake of higher consciousness and continue to chew on the teething biscuits of spiritual infancy.

All this is the mercy of God and the steps to higher evolution, but it can take a great deal of confusion and misery before we learn that. And some never do in this life and have to return and face the dilemma in a future life, or lives. Exoteric religion is not only not a help in such a time, it actually retards understanding of what is going on, and sometimes prevents it altogether.

The surest cure for this internal agony is steady yoga practice.

> **This is a great error and a bad sign. For a true lover of God loves him or the Eternal Goodness alike, in having and in not having, in sweetness and bitterness, in good or evil report, and the like, for he seeks alone the honor of God, and not his own, either in spiritual or natural things.**

This is very true; but how many people love God truly, and how many of them love God intelligently? The human condition itself is the *mahato bhayat*, the great terror the Bhagavad Gita (2:40) speaks about. Certainly all pass through this awful phase, but it is a horrible experience.

> **And therefore he stands alike unshaken in all things, at all seasons. Hereby let every man prove himself, how he stands towards God, his Creator and Lord.**

This is all true, but one thing is missing in this section and in the entire book: *how it is to be done.* Knowing what is wrong counts for very little if we do not know how to correct it. And even the author of this book does not tell us the way to spiritual success. Maybe he would have been burned at the stake if he had.

Since I am not in danger of the inquisitorial fires I have already told you and will say so again: "Be a yogi" (Bhagavad Gita 6:46). And how to do that I have explained in my book, *Soham Yoga: the Yoga of the Self.*

HADES AND HEAVEN

(CHAPTER ELEVEN)

Christ's soul must needs descend into hades, before it ascended into heaven. So must also the soul of man. But mark you in what manner this comes to pass.

The restoration which Christ Jesus incarnated to effect included every aspect of this world, including those who had lived in this world and now were in the astral world. "Hades" does not mean the place(s) of suffering for the expiation of karma, but the entire world of the departed. Saint Peter tell us that Jesus "went and preached unto the spirits in prison; which sometime were disobedient, when once the longsuffering of God waited in the days of Noah, while the ark was a preparing, wherein few, that is, eight souls were saved by water" (I Peter 3:19-20). Since Jesus was Noah in a previous life (see *Robe of Light*), those to whom he had preached before the flood were his spiritual charges, so he went into the realm where they were imprisoned and set them free to rise to higher life both back on the earth and in the astral regions. However, it has also been the accepted belief in both Eastern and Western Christianity that Jesus went into all the worlds of the departed and opened the way to higher evolution for them.

The Frankfurter is telling us that just as Jesus descended to help the bound souls, so each one of us must descend into our inner depths and turn our inner bondage of karma and the conditionings of prior incarnations into means for ascension in consciousness. That is, we must face and experience and transmute all that binds us, fulfilling the divine counsel: "be ye transformed by the renewing of your mind" (Romans 12:2). We must bring about our own transfiguration. Then like Jesus we will be enabled to ascend to the realms of the blessed.

Putting it more plainly, each one of us as yogis keep moving between inner hades and inner heaven as we bring about the transmutation of our bodies and their subtle energies. The stronger we become in spirit the more we can face and dissolve or transmute. Naturally, everyone wants to simply sail upward and onward into the divine kingdom and be permanently established in positive experience and development. But it does not work that way. One of the ways we neutralize negative karma is to go into the lions' den like Daniel and master them.

"Then the king commanded, and they brought Daniel, and cast him into the den of lions. Now the king spake and said unto Daniel, Thy God whom thou servest continually, he will deliver thee.... Then the king arose very early in the morning, and went in haste unto the den of lions. And when he came to the den, he cried with a lamentable voice unto Daniel: and the king spake and said to Daniel, O Daniel, servant of the living God, is thy God, whom thou servest continually, able to deliver thee from the lions? Then said Daniel unto the king, O king, live for ever. My God hath sent his angel, and hath shut the lions' mouths, that they have not hurt me: forasmuch as before him innocency was found in me; and also before thee, O king, have I done no hurt. Then was the king exceeding glad for him, and commanded that they should take Daniel up out of the den. So Daniel was taken up out of the den, and no manner of hurt was found upon him, because he believed in his God" (Daniel 6:16, 19-23).

The fact is, we go in and out of the lions' den and the king's palace until all negative karma and traits have been dissolved and we become established in their opposites.

We do not particularly enjoy the process, but that has no significance. "Verily I say unto thee, Thou shalt by no means come out thence, till thou hast paid the uttermost farthing" (Matthew 5:26). There are no exceptions. It is good to remember the words of Isaac Watts the hymnographer:

Must I be carried to the skies
    On flowery beds of ease?
While others fought to win the prize,
    And sailed through bloody seas?

Are there no foes for me to face?
　　Must I not stem the flood?
Is this vile world a friend to grace,
　　To help me on to God?

Sure I must fight, if I would reign–
　　Increase my courage, Lord!
I'll bear the toil, endure the pain,
　　Supported by Thy word.

Thy saints, in all this glorious war,
　　Shall conquer, though they die;
They view the triumph from afar,
　　And seize it with their eye.

When that illustrious day shall rise,
　　And all Thy armies shine
In robes of victory through the skies,
　　The glory shall be Thine.

This is why Jesus plainly told his disciples: "Whosoever doth not bear his cross, and come after me, cannot be my disciple. For which of you, intending to build a tower, sitteth not down first, and counteth the cost, whether he have sufficient to finish it? Lest haply, after he hath laid the foundation, and is not able to finish it, all that behold it begin to mock him, saying, This man began to build, and was not able to finish. Or what king, going to make war against another king, sitteth not down first, and consulteth whether he be able with ten thousand to meet him that cometh against him with twenty thousand? Or else, while the other is yet a great way off, he sendeth an ambassage, and desireth conditions of peace. So likewise, whosoever he be of you that forsaketh not all that he hath, he cannot be my disciple" (Luke 14:27-33).

And one of the things we must forsake is comfort and complacency.

Nothing grieves him but his own guilt and wickedness; for that is not right and is contrary to God, and for that cause he is grieved and troubled in spirit.

There are people who are angry, frustrated and opposed to countless things around them. They are continually wasting their life force by being "offended" and "outraged"–and thereby distracting themselves from that which is real and viable. The wise man regrets his own negativity and wrong actions, not wallowing in self-loathing (which is egotism) but keenly feeling the need to purify, control and change himself for the better. All "sin" is against his true, divine nature and against the Divine Being in which he lives, moves and has his individual being (Acts 17:28). Wishing to be in perfect union with God, he is intellectually (not emotionally) grieved and troubled and resolves to correct and change himself. He is aware of himself, but he is looking to God as his prime focus so he can embody the words of Saint Paul: "We all, with open face beholding as in a glass the glory of the Lord, are changed into the same image from glory to glory, even as by the Spirit of the Lord" (II Corinthians 3:18).

This is what is meant by true repentance for sin.

The word poorly translated "repent" in the Gospels is *metanoeo*, which means to totally change, to turn around one hundred and eighty degrees and face the other way. As Buddha said: "Turn around and lo! the other shore" of Nirvana. Most people's faces are never turned from the material world and rebirth, but the yogi's is turned toward spirit and eternal life in which the bonds of rebirth are broken forever. *Metanoeo* implies a permanent change extending into the future. It further means a change based on insight and intelligence, not emotion such as fear. As my first spiritual teacher, my Aunt Faye, often told me: "You can't make God a fire escape; you can only go toward him in love and he will do the same toward you." She had learned many years before that ignorant religion with its threats of judgment and hell could never enable anyone to truly change and move toward God.

And he who in this Present time enters into this hades, enters afterward into the Kingdom of Heaven, and obtains a foretaste there of which excels all the delight and joy which he ever has had or could have in this present time from temporal things.

Those who turn within in meditation and face their inner ignorance and negativity ("hades") will find that in time it melts away and is transmuted into positive consciousness and spiritual realization: the interior state of heaven. In this way he learns to desire and love the things of spirit and to disregard utterly the perishable things of not just this world but of all worlds in which rebirth is the law.

Now God has not forsaken a man in this hades, but he is laying his hand upon him, that the man may not desire nor regard anything but the Eternal Good only, and may come to know that that is so noble and passing good, that none can search out or express its bliss, consolation and joy, peace, rest and satisfaction.

Although life in this world is death and destruction without spirit-consciousness, awareness of that is the call of God to higher life in him. The suffering we undergo in this world is a call to awakening, not punishment or abandonment by God. "The sufferings of this present time are not worthy to be compared with the glory which shall be revealed in us" (Romans 8:18). All we need do is truly repent: turn around and begin the journey back to God, which is not a journey in time and space, but in our own consciousness. That is why Jesus told us: "Repent: for *the kingdom of heaven is at hand*" (Matthew 4:17), "Behold, the kingdom of God is within you" (Luke 17:21).

And then, when the man neither cares for, nor seeks, nor desires, anything but the Eternal Good alone, and seeks not himself, nor his own things, but the honor of God only, he is made a partaker of all manner of joy, bliss, peace, rest and consolation, and so the man is henceforth in the Kingdom of Heaven.

Again, it is all a matter of subjective awareness, the disposition of our inmost existence. Those who look outward will never find that which by its nature is inward. This is why exoteric religion is as meaningless and destructive as the world—it is part of the world, a child of the world. Only esoteric religion reveals the kingdom within, and yoga is the supreme esoteric religion.

This hades and this heaven are two good, safe ways for a man in this present time, and happy is he who truly finds them.

For this hades shall pass away,
But heaven shall endure for aye.

Ups and downs though they be, when they are the result of descending into hades to clear out the long-buried debris of our minds and of the consequent ascension brought about by that purification, we are completely safe and can be assured that progress is ours for the continued doing, that in time the purging will end and the ascension will become the norm, going higher and higher until there are no more such things as up and down, high or low, just the Now in which alone there is salvation (II Corinthians 6:2).

And when a man is in one of these two states, all is right with him, and he is as safe in hades as in heaven. Therefore he shall never forget either of them, but lay up the remembrance of them in his heart.

When I was a child, people in our small town would occasionally say to one another: "Let's go over and listen to how Colonel Burge [my maternal grandfather] won the Spanish-American War!" For old soldiers love to tell about their war experiences. In the same way we will not forget the struggle along the way to Peace. However, we will be more grateful for its ending than for its striving. And will be satisfied if only we and God remember the saga.

The Peace of Christ

(Chapter Twelve)

Many say they have no peace nor rest, but so many crosses and trials, afflictions and sorrows, that they know not how they shall ever get through them. Now he who in truth will perceive and take note, perceives clearly, that true peace and rest lie not in outward things; for if it were so, the Evil Spirit also would have peace when things go according to his will, which is nowise the case; for the prophet declares, "There is no peace, saith my God, to the wicked." (Isaiah 57:21).

The most important point in this is the fact that since "true peace and rest lie not in outward things" then it is evident that outward things cannot disturb the true peace which is always within us and in which we need to establish ourselves through spiritual cultivation, especially meditation.

And therefore we must consider and see what is that peace which Christ left to his disciples at the last, when he said: "Peace I leave with you, my peace I give unto you" (John 14:27).

We may perceive that in these words Christ did not mean a bodily and outward peace; for his beloved disciples, with all his friends and followers, have ever suffered, from the beginning, great affliction, persecution, nay, often martyrdom, as Christ himself said: "In the world ye shall have tribulation" (John 16:33).

Yet the saints have demonstrated for two thousand years that peace profound is possible even in the midst of the raging storms of earthly experience. In prison they have sung with joy and in torture they have rested content in their spirit which no bodily torment could touch.

But Christ meant that true, inward peace of the heart, which begins here, and endures for ever hereafter.

The peace of eternal life is not to be attained after death, but is to be laid hold of even in this world. Certainly it will increase the higher we rise in the various subtle worlds until we reach perfection, but as the Frankfurter says, it begins here. If we do not find it here we will not find it elsewhere.

Therefore he said: "Not as the world giveth," for the world is false, and deceives in her gifts. She promises much, and performs little.

Anyone who does not know this already has been living with eyes and ears shut. The truth is, the world gives nothing, but promises and never fulfills (rather like the carrot dangling in front of the horse or donkey), or hands it to us and snatches it back like the old wallet-on-a-string prank. On occasion the world proposes a trade, promising material things if we will abandon our spiritual principles. Then once we agree, the world hands it over and grabs it back almost immediately. I have seen this happen very much, and never was the dupe able to regain the spiritual wealth he had given away. Emptiness was the result of his bad bargain.

Moreover there lives no man on earth who may always have rest and peace without troubles and crosses, with whom things always go according to his will; there is always something to be suffered here, turn which way you will. And as soon as you are quit of one assault, perhaps two come in its place. Wherefore yield yourself willingly to them, and seek only that true peace of the heart, which none can take away from thee, that you mayest overcome all assaults.

We are not being told to melt into a puddle of cowardly passivity, but are given the positive life plan of paying minimal attention to troubles and problems and keep our eyes fixed on the goal of life eternal in God. As we used to sing when I was a child:

> Just trust Him and be true,
> And see what He will do,
> He'll never disappoint your soul;
> When you have done your best,
> Let Jesus do the rest,
> And keep your eyes upon the goal.

Here, too, meditation is indispensible.

> **Thus then, Christ meant that inward peace which can break through all assaults and crosses of oppression, suffering, misery, humiliation and what more there may be of the like, so that a man may be joyful and patient therein, like the beloved disciples and followers of Christ.**

The peace of our inner Christ is a mighty power that truly "can break through" all that comes into our life. "Who shall separate us from the love of Christ? shall tribulation, or distress, or persecution, or famine, or nakedness, or peril, or sword? As it is written, For thy sake we are killed all the day long; we are accounted as sheep for the slaughter. Nay, in all these things we are more than conquerors through him that loved us. For I am persuaded, that neither death, nor life, nor angels, nor principalities, nor powers, nor things present, nor things to come, nor height, nor depth, nor any other creature, shall be able to separate us from the love of God, which is in Christ Jesus our Lord." (Romans 8:35-39). "Be strong in the Lord, and in the power of his might" (Ephesians 6:10). "Be strong in the grace that is in Christ Jesus" (II Timothy 2:1).

Now he who will in love give his whole diligence and might thereto, will verily come to know that true eternal peace which is God himself, as far as it is possible to a creature; insomuch that what was bitter to him before, shall become sweet, and his heart shall remain unmoved under all changes, at all times, and after this life, he shall attain unto everlasting peace.

Here is the pinnacle of this chapter: *True eternal peace is God himself.* What we are seeking for is no less than union with God, total and perfect union in which we are possessed by God and God is possessed by us.

TOO MUCH TOO SOON

(CHAPTER THIRTEEN)

Childish egos overestimate their abilities, value and significance. This is one of the fundamental troubles of the human race: lack of adult personalities. Consequently everything is distorted in the minds of what is rather frighteningly called "society at large," evoking images of Frankenstein's monster wandering around and ravaging whatever comes to hand. Over and over we see "advances" that are really huge setbacks. Nearly every supposed improvement is a form of damage or ruin. This situation is present in contemporary religion that is so out of touch with reality that it is no wonder some people conclude that to be religious is to be crazy. Blessed are the few who know their limitations and what they are and what they are not. Seeing this clearly seven centuries ago, the Teutonic priest-knight has something to say on the matter.

> **Tauler says: "There be some men at the present time, who take leave of types and symbols too soon, before they have drawn out all the truth and instruction contained therein." Hence they are scarcely or perhaps never able to understand the truth aright.**

This is an extremely interesting statement. The Frankfurter is telling us that the very first step in understanding spiritually inspired writings is instruction in symbolism, in learning to see through or beyond the literal or physical into the metaphysical. All true religion is mysticism, and its principles often have to be conveyed in the symbolic language of mysticism. Without knowledge of this language, grave errors in interpretation will occur.

There is a certain personality type that takes pride in always being literal in determining the meaning of scriptures. The fact is, they simply have no imagination. (And are usually suffering from anxiety neurosis.) One of the reasons that Jesus said: "Whosoever shall not receive the kingdom of God as a little child shall in no wise enter therein" (Luke 18:17), was the need for a "magical consciousness" to penetrate the mysteries revealed by authentic religion, a consciousness that is found in children whose past life karmas have not obscured it. When we encounter those who lack this mystical outlook there is very little good to be accomplished by speaking with them. We should be polite to them but expect nothing much to come of any communication. Yet in time all will be well. Both we and God have time to wait. Meanwhile, "keep your eyes upon the goal."

For such men will follow no one, and lean unto their own understandings, and desire to fly before they are fledged.

As someone once said: "The trouble with ignorance is that it picks up confidence as it goes along." Religious movements are founded by such people and then destroyed by the same kind of people. And worthy, sincere people often find themselves in the middle.

I once read of a university that asked applicants' parents to fill out a personal profile of the applicant. One question was: "Is he/she a good leader?" One parent wrote: "He is not a leader at all, but is a very good follower." Immediately a letter came from the university saying: "Your son is accepted. We have already enrolled a few hundred leaders and desperately need at least one follower."

I think perhaps the most telling symptom of our time regarding these kind that want to fly before being hatched, is the way in which organizations of all types (especially yoga organizations) offer Teacher Training programs but nothing for beginners. I remember being at a meditation center in Canada when a man walked in and announced: "I want to be an Initiator." There are plenty of groups that accommodate such personalities—and usually are being run by them as well. In the heyday of one such group their main propaganda slogan was the sentence: "You need believe in no God beyond yourself," or variations on that theme. Many yoga groups made a point of saying that no one needed to believe in God to practice their methods. But everyone had to pay money to learn them!!! "For where your treasure is, there your heart will be also" (Matthew 6:21).

They would fain mount up to heaven in one flight; albeit Christ did not so, for after his resurrection, he remained full forty days with his beloved disciples.

Once in my early yogi-sadhu days a young man said to me: "I don't want to spend of lot of time on it, but couldn't you tell me in just about five minutes your whole philosophy?" Considering he had grown up in a church that did not have enough belief or discipline to fill up a five minutes' exposition, I understood. But I also told him it could not be done about mine.

One of my favorite religious cartoons showed a drunk lying in the gutter and saying to a Salvation Army woman who is bending over him: "Can you save me here, or do I have to go somewhere?" I have encountered quite a few groups whose founder attained enlightenment in less than a week. One leader's autobiography assured the reader that she had quickly and effortlessly attained cosmic consciousness at the very beginning of her search and had gone on from there. She most certainly *had* gone on.

I was born in the great days of radio when television was just a rumor. The one drawback was that when you turned on a radio you had to wait for the tubes to warm up before you heard anything. And the older the tubes the longer you waited. I knew one family that had to turn on their radio several minutes before the program they wanted to hear came on. So you can imagine what it was like when my father came home with a radio that spoke the moment you turned it on. I kept turning it on and off, amazed at such an achievement. And I did not accept the existence of LP records until I saw and heard one for myself.

But in our time instant response and instant gratification are demanded. Or else. Today I downloaded *Anna Bolena* from Amazon.com. Before the download was complete I already had gotten an email thanking me for my order. I love it when things work that way in material life, but I assure you it does not work that way in spiritual life. (Though I have met my share of yogis who had enough psychic energy to zap and impress prospective customers at the first encounter.) The guru trap yawns wide, awaiting those seeking quick and easy enlightenment. A few months before I went to India I sent away for instructions in "the easiest, quickest and cheapest way to God-realization." I just had to know what it was. It was pretty funny, actually.

No one can be made perfect in a day.

The truth is we cannot be *made* perfect, ever, because we already *are* perfect. But we have forgotten it and strayed far away into the jungle of delusion. And we cannot find our way back to our eternal perfection in a single day. Karma stands in the way. What we have done we must undo. Every dent we have put in our mind has to be pounded out. We made the mess and we must clean it up, because in the cleaning we correct ourself. Yoga is the knowledge we need to straighten things out.

A man must begin by denying himself, and willingly forsaking all things for God's sake, and must give up his own will, and all his natural inclinations, and separate and cleanse himself thoroughly from all sins and evil ways.

Basically we have to acknowledge our culpability for the kind of life we find ourselves in. Since ego is at the bottom *and* the top, there is a positive kind of self-renunciation that is a freeing of ourselves from the bonds of ego. Seeking God and conforming ourselves to the way of God while avoiding "our" ways of ignorance and evil is a full time occupation.

Since we only know our delusive ego and not our true Self which is immortal, eternal spirit, we must forsake the ego and its ways and find our Self at the bottom of the deep pit where it has been buried deeper and deeper in each previous life.

After this, let him humbly take up the cross and follow Christ.

The cross is not an instrument of torture and death, it is a balance by means of which we can progress from duality to unity, from confusion to peace.

We need a good look at the cross–not the crucifix, but the cross itself. First of all, it is not the t-shape we are used to seeing. According to Therese Neumann the stigmatist, the cross of Jesus was made of three pieces: a long center shaft and a left and right arm that were not level but turned up at an angle. This is the exact sign or symbol of the sacred Triveni in north central India where the three most sacred rivers, Saraswati, Jumna and Ganges, meet. The magnetism of this junction is indescribable, and to be immersed (baptized) at that point is a profound purification never to be forgotten. This is where sins are buried and souls come to life. I am not exaggerating. I have experienced it.

Furthermore, this triple figure is a symbol of the entire makeup of the human being. The central, longest shaft represents the spirit, the left piece represents the body and the right piece the mind. And it is also a symbol of the Holy Trinity, the central part being the Father and the two extensions the Son (right) and Holy Spirit (left).

It is this cross, the consciousness of our true Self and our divine Source, that we must take up and follow on the way of Christ to become revealed sons of God. Then we will truly be Christians–other Christs.

Also let him take and receive example and instruction, reproof, counsel and teaching from devout and perfect servants of God, and not follow his own guidance.

"Sharp as the edge of a razor and hard to cross, difficult to tread is that path [so] sages declare" (Katha Upanishad 1:3:14). This is because the aspirant must always be balancing himself on the razor's edge. It is dangerous to believe everything we are told, and it is dangerous to doubt everything we are told. Sometimes one attitude is necessary, and at other times a different approach is needed. Sri Ramakrishna often said that even the scriptures contain a mixture of sand and sugar. The wise man takes the sugar, leaving aside the sand. But this is not easy; it requires great skill born of intense spiritual discipline (tapasya). We should certainly examine the teachings of the "wise," but we must use our intelligence and experience as well.

In India I always had to use my head. People whom I respected greatly more than once told me utter nonsense. I was often told something was true that was not at all true; and I was often told that certain things were not true that I knew absolutely were true. It would have been much more comfortable and secure just accepting everything I heard, but that was the path to real trouble. It is just as possible for good and sincere people to be mistaken as for anyone else. I learned this the hard way.

Therefore the seeker should find out what the wise and the holy have said on a subject and then cautiously proceed to sift the sugar from the sand. And there is a lot more sand than sugar. The author is right in advising us to get the teachings of "devout and perfect servants of God," but who will decide for us who is devout and perfect? Ultimately we will have to decide for ourself. Those who are not willing to take chances and risks will end up nowhere. Of course the best plan is to become devout and perfect ourselves.

A Zen master taught for many years: The Buddha is the Mind. One day he called in a disciple and told him: "I have realized that all these years I was wrong. The truth is: No Buddha, No Mind." He then told the disciple to seek out one of his earlier disciples who lived far away in a mountain range and tell him of the change in the Master's teaching. The disciple managed to find the hermit and told him that the Master now taught No Buddha, No Mind, so he should change his belief. "Well, I still say The Buddha is the Mind," responded the hermit. Fueled by indignation the disciple went running back to the Master and told him: "When I found him, I informed that hermit he should henceforth believe No Buddha, No Mind, as you now teach. And he had the temerity to say that he still believed The Buddha is the Mind!" The Master smiled and said: "I see he has attained maturity."

Thus the work shall be established and come to a good end.

Tradition is an important part of spiritual knowledge, but ignorance has been around a long time and is often thought to be a venerable tradition. Whom can you trust? Only those who are worthy of trust. And how will you know who is worthy? By close scrutiny and relying on your own good sense and experience. There is no absolutely safe guide either inside or outside. You do your best and use your intelligence. As Paramhansa Nityananda pointed out, we were born with a brain, not a book. But we were born with an eternal and unbreakable connection to God. That is good to remember.

> **And when a man has thus broken loose from and outleaped all temporal things and creatures, he may afterwards become perfect in a life of contemplation.**

One of the great problems in contemporary life is our thinking that something is the end of the path when it is really only the beginning, or often just the chance of beginning the beginning. So divesting ourselves of "all temporal things and creatures" is not some great attainment, but just the possibility that we may after great endeavor become perfect in the yoga life and become yoga siddhas.

Rome was not built in a day nor could Rome be dismantled in a day. At one point following is good, but eventually we must strike out on our own and hack our own way through the jungle.

> **For he who will have the one must let the other go. There is no other way.**

Either we will possess temporal things or we will possess eternal things. Either we will have temporal knowledge or eternal knowledge. Either we will ourselves be either temporal or eternal. Never both. The path to the eternal leads away from the temporal, and the way to the temporal leads away from the eternal. "Choose you this day whom ye will serve" (Joshua 24:15). "It is written in the prophets, And they shall be all taught of God" (John 6:45).

THREE STEPS TO GOD

(CHAPTER FOURTEEN)

Now be assured that no one can be enlightened unless he be first cleansed or purified and stripped. So also, no one can be united with God unless he be first enlightened. Thus there are three stages: first, the purification; secondly, the enlightening; thirdly, the union.

These three steps to God-realization are found in the writings of Saint Dionysius the Areopagite, the disciple of Saint Paul whom he encountered on Mars Hill when the Apostle spoke to the philosophers of Athens (Acts 17:16-34). In English writings they are usually referred to as the purgative, illuminative and unitive states. They always occur in this order: first, perfect purification; second, perfect illumination of the intellect; and third, perfect and total union with God, in which not one atom of the person's being remains untouched and, yes, unsummed (unabsorbed) by God. Such a one can truthfully say: "I live; yet not I, but Christ liveth in me" (Galatians 2:20). For: "when that which is perfect is come, then that which is in part shall be done away" (I Corinthians 13:10).

The Frankfurter now gives us information on the practical side of these three states.

The purification concerns those who are beginning or repenting, and is brought to pass in a threefold wise; by contrition and sorrow for sin, by full confession, by hearty amendment.

As already pointed out in the commentary on chapter eleven, "repentance" really means "reformation" in the sense of a complete turnabout on all levels–not just the external, because that usually ends in hypocrisy.

Contrition and sorrow for sin. Many "sinners" whine and mope a lot, thinking that is repentance and that those who see them playing penitent will accept that as real change, when it is not that at all: just ego display to cover up the lack of reformation. Real contrition and sorrow are deep regret of past deeds and a strong resolve to change for the better. It is a matter of intelligent will, not emotion which is the ego's domain most of the time. That is why Saint Paul wrote: "Godly sorrow worketh repentance to salvation not to be repented of: but the sorrow of the world worketh death." (II Corinthians 7:10). It is pretty simple: if we truly change and do not slip back into our old ways, then our sorrow or regret are positive and sincere. But if it is just ego display, "sorrow of the world," then further degeneration can be expected (guaranteed, actually).

Full confession. This is full acknowledgement of our wrongdoings and negative states of mind. It is totally admitting what is wrong with us and setting about to correct it. This is both self-honesty and honesty with others. No fudging and no denial. Those who say: "That was another person," or "I am a different person now" are usually incorrigible. Sociopaths never admit responsibility or guilt, though they may fake admission on occasion. Another sign of insincere "repentance" is exaggerated repentance and voluble self-castigation, along with a ridiculous exaggeration of the gravity of the wrongdoing. For example, if they swat a fly they claim to have committed murder; if they shortchange someone a little bit they carry on like they committed armed robbery. This is an attempt to bamboozle. This truly is the way of the sociopath.

Hearty amendment. From the heart! Sincere and willing admission and reformation–actually, gladness at being able to clear themselves. For when the load is gone, the heart is lighter. True repentance is not bitter medicine but healing balm and the cause of eventual rejoicing.

Cleansed or purified and stripped. Ridding ourselves of all that hinders our ascent in inner and outer life is the prime requisite for real spiritual change and elevation in consciousness. It is drastic, but absolutely necessary. And results in peace and joy.

The enlightening belongs to such as are growing, and also takes place in three ways: to wit, by the eschewal of sin, by the practice of virtue and good works, and by the willing endurance of all manner of temptation and trials.

The enlightening belongs to such as are growing. Evolution is the only path to enlightenment. We *grow* into wisdom and holiness. All authentic spiritual growth is gradual and intentional, even methodical. The idea of instant salvation, of lightning-strike conversion that accomplishes everything in the wink of an eye, is self-delusive mythology, and Fundamentalist Protestantism is based on this delusion. I do not mean that real change cannot occur seemingly in a moment, but if studied it will be seen that the change has gradually come from growth, that it has a definite genealogy, and has been coming on for some time, though the person may not have been aware of it. This is how children pass into adulthood. The change is slow, but one day to their surprise they find childhood is over. It seems instant, but is no such thing. A bishop who had a medical degree once told me a very important principle: all extremely rapid or instant growth or change in the body is pathological in character. And that can be applied to spiritual life as well.

The eschewal of sin. A firm and flat-footed resistance to all that is negative is a requisite for spiritual insight and growth. STOP–Not Just Slow, is the only way. "Hating sin" gets no one anywhere but worse off. It is love of virtue and the path to God that keeps us moving on in the right way.

The practice of virtue and good works. As Buddha proclaimed, Right Action is an essential of the path that leads to enlightenment. Like anything else that gets results, virtue is a matter of *practice*, of *doing*. It is the intelligent application of will. The creation of positive karma by such action is the aspirant's safeguard as well as a means of dissolving negative karma.

The willing endurance of all manner of temptation and trials. All that comes or happens to us is a matter of karma; there no chance or caprice in life. We reap what we have sown. We cannot reap what has not been sown. Simple; but people have a hard time facing it.

The wise know that nothing is "luck" or "fate," but the purely mathematical response of the universe to their own past action. The old nonsense of "life's lottery" that certain manipulative politicians love to bandy about is just that: nonsense. Errant nonsense, actually. It, too, is the way of the sociopath. There are no innocent victims; there is no injustice in the universe. Quite the opposite, there is only justice and the revelation of the true nature of things, including people. Karma; karma; karma. The wise never forget that.

> **The union belongs to such as are perfect, and also is brought to pass in three ways: to wit, by pureness and singleness of heart, by love, and by the contemplation of God, the Creator of all things.**

As pointed out before, in the Gospels, the Greek word translated "perfect" is *teleios*, which means to be complete in the sense of being finished, completed with nothing more remaining to be done or gained. In other words, the perfect are those who have totally evolved "unto the measure of the stature of the fulness of Christ" (Ephesians 4:13). "At the end of many births the wise man takes refuge in me. He knows: All is Vasudeva. How very rare is that great soul" (Bhagavad Gita 7:19).

Pureness and singleness of heart. A heart purified totally and freed of all conflict and contradiction, united in perfect orientation toward God and the life in God: this is one of the three characteristics of those perfectly united with God.

Love. God is love (I John 4:8), and so are his children. Neither God nor his offspring (Acts 17:28) have any other motive or purpose but this divine love.

> Could we with ink the ocean fill,
> And were the skies of parchment made,
> Were every stalk on earth a quill,
> And every man a scribe by trade;

To write the love of God above
Would drain the ocean dry;
Nor could the scroll contain the whole,
Though stretched from sky to sky.

Oh, love of God, how rich and pure!
How measureless and strong!
It shall forevermore endure–
The saints' and angels' song.

The contemplation of God. "Blessed are the pure in heart: for they shall see God" (Matthew 5:8). To *see* God is to *be* God; this is the secret of the great ones, those who have become perfect in God. The sole purpose of the devotee's life is total union with God.

"Beloved, now are we the sons of God, and it doth not yet appear what we shall be: but we know that, when he shall appear, we shall be like him; for we shall see him as he is. And every man that hath this hope in him purifieth himself, even as he is pure." (I John 3:2-3).

THE DEATH OF DEATH AND
THE LIFE OF LIFE

(CHAPTER FIFTEEN)

All that in Adam fell and died, was raised again and made alive in Christ, and all that rose up and was made alive in Adam, fell and died in Christ.

That which is called "the fall of man" did not take place on earth but in the astral world just above the material plane. Adam and Eve were not perfect, but they had tremendous spiritual potential and possessed spiritual senses that enabled them to communicate with very high spiritual beings. They were also utterly innocent of evil or malice. Clothed in light, they were ready for higher consciousness. Having only elemental human minds they were incapable of "sin" in the full-blown sense, but they did indeed fall short and fail. This failure entailed the loss of their Paradise light-body and opening to the possibility of further transgressing their potential status. This psychic trauma impelled them back and downward to the earth where they entered material bodies once more with their attendant ills of limitation of consciousness and susceptibility to further degradation and confusion. (For a fuller understanding of this, see *Robe of Light*.)

That which they lost, to which they "died," was restored by and in Jesus and imparted to the children of Adam. But quickly the internal means of further purification and growth were lost to Christianity and exoteric theology blocked and blinded Christians to the ways of divine sonship. As a result, today we have the incredible shambles called Christianity, which is not Christianity at all, but anti-Christianity. For if there is no esoteric understanding, and if its effects are not carried onward through interior cultivation by practice of yoga meditation, a terrible bottleneck results and rebirth is virtually the only possible fate for those whom Jesus came to set free. That is why Jesus asked his disciples: "When the Son of man cometh [again], shall he find faith on the earth?" (Luke 18:8). Churchianity prevails throughout the world, but where is Christianity to be found? The words of Saint James to Churchianity as it was starting in his day certainly apply: "Your riches are corrupted, and your garments are motheaten. Your gold and silver is cankered; and the rust of them shall be a witness against you, and shall eat your flesh as it were fire" (James 5:2-3). Nevertheless, Jesus will return to earth in a new incarnation and things will go better. And for those that become yogis right now there will be no need to wait, for Christ shall be manifested in us.

But what was that? I answer, true obedience and disobedience.

Obedience and disobedience are really not very good words in this place because they carry with them the exoteric view of humanity and its dilemma. It is better to say that we are considering conformity to the evolutionary plan of the cosmos and non-conformity to that plan: following the Law and transgressing the Law. This is what our life is all about: living in accordance with our true nature and its inherent potentials or living in violation of our true nature and frustrating its inherent potentials.

It is just that simple. We make ourselves happy or miserable according to whether we cooperate with our inmost impulse to divinization or defy and contravene it. In other words, we either glorify ourselves or we destroy ourselves. It is incredible that people so often choose the harmful and the deadly, but it is because of basic ignorance and addiction to that which ruins our chances even more. And ignorant religion actively supports our misperceptions and leads us even further astray.

We are the problem. That is why Krishna says: "One should uplift oneself by the lower self; one should not degrade oneself. The lower self can truly be a friend of the lower self, and the lower self alone can be an enemy of the lower self. For him who has conquered himself by the lower self, the lower self is a friend. But for him who has not conquered himself, the lower self remains hostile, like an enemy" (Bhagavad Gita 6:5-6). This brings to mind the memorable statement of Pogo Possum: "We have met the enemy and he is us."

> But what is true obedience? I answer, that a man should so stand free, being quit of himself, that is, of his I, and Me, and Self, and Mine, and the like, that in all things, he should no more seek or regard himself, than if he did not exist, and should take as little account of himself as if he were not, and another had done all his works.

This gives me a chill because I am aware that it might almost always be misinterpreted as a statement that we are nothing, less than nothing and totally worthless. But something completely different is the real meaning: that we should be so intent on God and our spirit-Self, that all else seems but shifting shadows without substance or ultimate value. It is not an expression of self-loathing or self-castigation, but insight into the glory and wonder that is spirit, individual and cosmic. Everything else is seen as merely childish and fundamentally non-existent. "When I was a child, I spake as a child, I understood as a child, I thought as a child: but when I became a man, I put away childish things" (I Corinthians 13:11). This is the right perspective, the perspective of a spiritual adult, a view unclouded or distorted by ego which by its nature is viciously childish, not at all unlike Rhoda in *The Bad Seed* (played by Patty MacCormack in the motion picture).

Likewise he should count all the creatures for nothing.

All that is temporal is unsatisfying because it is antithetical to our eternal, divine nature. The problem is not that we are sinners, but that we are gods deluded into acting like sinners and believing in sin and death rather than in truth and life. We need to see the true worthlessness of all things that are relative, changing and ultimately perishable.

What is there then, which is, and which we may count for somewhat? I answer, nothing but that which we may call God.

We must realize that the Creator is of infinite worth–as are we, since we derive our existence from him. We must live in the Spirit exclusively.

Behold! this is very obedience in the truth, and thus it will be in a blessed eternity. There nothing is sought nor thought of, nor loved, but the one thing only.

This goal is not easy, but it is simple considering that our attention need be fixed on one thing only: the Absolute. And this is done immediately and continuously through the practice of Soham Yoga Sadhana. (See *Soham Yoga: The Yoga of the Self, Light of Soham* and *The Inspired Wisdom of Sri Gajanana Maharaj.*)

Hereby we may mark what disobedience is: to wit, that a man makes some account of himself, and thinks that he is, and knows, and can do somewhat, and seeks himself and his own ends in the things around him, and has regard to and loves himself, and the like.

This is a very complete description that can be summed up in these words: total ego-involvement and total ego-interest. This is the history of each of us for many lifetimes until we come to understand that there is a lot more to life–and to us–than our ego.

Man is created for true obedience, and is bound of right to render it to God.

This is true because God is the very basis of our being, the essence of all we are. We speak of having a lower and a higher self, and that is true, but what we must come to know is that God is the infinite Higher Self of our finite higher self. To become absorbed in God is to fully know ourself, to attain the ultimate knowledge.

> **And this obedience fell and died in Adam, and rose again and lived in Christ. Yes, Christ's human nature was so utterly bereft of Self, and apart from all creatures, as no man's ever was, and was nothing else but "a house and habitation of God."**

It is crucial for us to realize that there is a false self and a real Self. Since our real Self is eternally united with God and is the means by which we come to know God, when reading statements about "self" we have to understand which of the two selfs is being considered. We are told in some writings that we must "abandon self." But our present dilemma is that we have abandoned our true Self and cling to the false self, the ego. Only when we distinguish between the true and the false can we benefit from the call to leave "self" behind and seek God.

Actually, much as I respect this book, there is no denying that the Frankfurter's problem in using these expressions is his background as a Western Christian theologian. He uses Western terms while meaning them in the Eastern sense. (I have found this in Eastern European Roman Catholic books, also.) It certainly is possible for exoteric Christians to read this book and interpret much of it according to current Western ideas about God and man, and they cannot be faulted if they consider that what I am writing is erroneous and a distortion. But it is not. Much of this book cannot be understood except as the East knows the things of the spirit to be.

Here is an example. From childhood we hear that Jesus died for our sins, and that is meant in the sense that Jesus died so we could be forgiven of our sins and not have to suffer their consequences; that he suffered in our place. But that is not so. Jesus died *because* of our sins, since as Adam he plunged the human race into its present condition which has gotten progressively worse in the passing of time. Therefore his "atoning death" on the cross was not to atone for *our* sins but to atone for *his* ancient transgression by which he opened for humanity the gates of sorrow, misery and death. Jesus died to atone for his karma incurred as Adam. To understand this better see *Robe of Light*.

> **Neither of that in him which belonged to God, nor of that which was a living human nature and a habitation of God, did he, as man, claim anything for his own.**

Here, again, the context of the unity of God and man must be kept in mind. Of course nothing is "of us," but the Frankfurter does not mean that we disregard and even despise "us" and "ourselves"–nor did Jesus. He means that since Jesus was totally one with God, like Swami Sivananda's poem he saw only God, not himself in the limited view which is the only one samsarins (wanderers in this world from birth to birth) know.

> **His human nature did not even take unto itself the Godhead, whose dwelling it was, nor anything that this same Godhead willed, or did or left undone in him, nor yet anything of all that his human nature did or suffered; but in Christ's human nature there was no claiming of anything, nor seeking nor desire, saving that what was due might be rendered to the Godhead, and he did not call this very desire his own.**

Read this carefully and realize that what is being described is the state of consciousness of every liberated being, or siddha. And if subsequent to their realization they enter any world for the uplift of others, they, too, are sons of God, incarnations of God Consciousness and saviors of those worlds. The great error of Christianity has been the insistence that Jesus was and is unique, when indeed he was the revelation of what every sentient being is destined to become. We may not see or recognize many such avatars in this material plane, but they are often here and occasionally appear openly. Countless more live in the higher worlds where they are seen, heard, known and followed. On earth we tend to kill or persecute them. But that is the nature of this world.

Of this matter no more can be said, or written here, for it is unspeakable, and was never yet and never will be fully uttered; for it can neither be spoken nor written but by him who is and knows its ground; that is, God himself, who can do all things well.

The Frankfurter himself was flirting with the fires of the Inquisition by writing this book and could easily have been burned as a heretic by the "orthodox."

THE OLD MAN AND THE NEW MAN

(CHAPTER SIXTEEN)

"Christ is risen from the dead, and become the firstfruits of them that slept. For since by man came death, by man came also the resurrection of the dead. For as in Adam all die, even so in Christ shall all be made alive" (I Corinthians 15:20-22).

Again, when we read of the old man and the new man we must mark what that means.

Saint Paul speaks of the "old man" and the "new man." Long before that, the philosopher-sages of India spoke of the "punyapurusha" and the "papapurusha," the "man of merit and virtue" and the "man of demerit and wrongdoing." Both are in us. Sri Ramakrishna saw his punyapurusha during his intense sadhana. Later he told people: "During my sadhana, when I meditated, I would actually see a person sitting next to me with a trident in his hand. He would threaten to strike me with the weapon unless I fixed my mind on the Lotus Feet of God, warning me that it would pierce my breast if my mind strayed from God." At another time he saw two men emerge from his body and fight one another. One was his papapurusha and the other was his punyapurusha. The punyapurusha killed the papapurusha with a trident, the weapon of Shiva. The meaning was that the positive side of Sri Ramakrishna was able to vanquish and destroy the negative side through the power of yoga (tapasya).

The same symbolism is found in the Bhagavad Gita where the body of the yogi is the field of battle and the Pandavas, the positive side of his nature, fight with the Kauravas, the negative side of his nature. In that battle both the positive and negative characteristics strive together, and just as in the actual battle of the Mahabharata nearly every one dies on both sides. The eldest Pandava, Yudhisthira, who was considered the perfect embodiment of dharma (righteousness), ascended bodily into the higher worlds, symbolizing that everything but the consciousness of pure spirit perishes and the Light of the Self alone remains. This is liberation (moksha). However, nothing is really lost because everything has come out of the Light of the Spirit and therefore everything is ours in that Light.

> **The old man is Adam and disobedience, the (ego-)Self, the Me, and so forth.**

The ego and all that goes to make up its dominion, including the negative karmas incurred by ego-based acts, is the old man, the Adam in which all die through the loss of spirit-consciousness that is itself the true Self (Atma).

> **But the new man is Christ and true obedience, a giving up and denying oneself of all temporal things, and seeking the honor of God alone in all things.**

Christhood is the awakening to the infinite life of the spirit and the casting aside of all that is not of the spirit and dwelling alone (centered) in the Christ Consciousness that is eternal life.

Those who follow the way of enlightenment come to realize that yoga is the real religion, for only yoga can reveal the inner Self, the inner Buddha or the inner Christ. Only the yogi can fully know the truth of religion, whatever name it may bear. We must first and foremost be yogis and adherents of a religion only secondarily—*very* secondarily. The great yogi Gorakhnath wrote: "By birth I am a Hindu; but by maturity I am a Yogi." That is why when yogis meet they recognize one another as kindred spirits and give little thought to each others' external religion. "With minds and lives intent on me, enlightening one another, and speaking of me constantly, they are content and rejoice in me. To them, the constantly steadfast, worshipping me with affection, I bestow the buddhi yoga by which they come to me" (Bhagavad Gita 10:9-10).

And when dying and perishing and the like are spoken of, it means that the old man should be destroyed, and not seek its own either in spiritual or in natural things.

This is the true Way of the Cross, not the morbid obsession with shedding of blood and death and seeking out suffering and humiliation. That is reverse-image egotism, profound spiritual and mental illness. The true Way of the Cross is the joyous ending of ego and all its attendant miseries and enslavements. It is not that we die, but that we finally come to life. We arise from death and stand forth in Life, boundless Life. This is the Communion of the Saints—nothing else.

For where this is brought about in a true divine light, there the new man is born again.

Yes!

In like manner, it has been said that man should die unto himself, that is, to earthly pleasures, consolations, joys, appetites, the I, the Self, and all that is thereof in man, to which he clings and on which he is yet leaning with content, and thinks much of.

Just think: we are addicted, even enslaved, to things that we cannot own or keep. In every life death sweeps us away from all we have been scrambling after and clinging to. Even that which we think is ourself cannot remain because it is just a mirage. Not learning this, we struggle throughout life after life seeking, finding and losing what we never really ever have. It is just like the experience I described in the commentary on Chapter Three when as a child I somehow had the idea that if I saw something in a dream that I wanted and held on to it, when I awoke I would have brought it over from my dream.

How hard it is to awaken from the childish dreams we have dreamed over and over. Awakening is the only thing that will help us; no other person or influence can do that; the awakening must come from within ourselves spontaneously. It is altogether a matter of growth, of evolution. There is nothing we can do for those who still sleep. We cannot wait for them to awaken, for that may be ages from now, especially since we sometimes waken for a brief time in our own lives and then fall right back to sleep. What should we do? We should start traveling the Highway to the Infinite right now and never look back, only forward.

Whether it be the man himself, or any other creature, whatever it be, it must depart and die, if the man is to be brought aright to another mind, according to the truth.

It is a favorite pastime of the sleepers and dreamers to ask over and over: "Why does God allow…?" The answer is that there is no other way to get us to awaken, to consciously and deliberately cast aside the follies of our dreamworld and awaken to present realities so we can possibly progress to higher realities. It is all about growth, and it comes about in its own good and right time. It cannot be hastened and it cannot be delayed, no matter how it may seem to us.

Regarding this Sri Ramakrishna said: "You must remember that nothing can be achieved except in its proper time. Some persons must pass through many experiences and perform many worldly duties before they can turn their attention to God; so they have to wait a long time. If an abscess is lanced before it is soft, the result is not good; the surgeon makes the opening when it is soft and has come to a head. Once a child said to its mother: 'Mother, I am going to sleep now. Please wake me up when I feel the call of nature.' 'My child,' said the mother, 'when it is time for that, you will wake up yourself. I shan't have to wake you.'" He also said: "I want you to remember this. You may impart thousands of instructions to people, but they will not bear fruit except in proper time."

So it is. Spiritual awakening does not come from outside but from within, from the core of our existence, the Self. No external factor can awaken us. First we must be inwardly developed to the point where we will make the right response to external factors. Then they will seem to awaken us, but it will all come from within. Otherwise, as I have said, we will wake for a short time and then lapse back into sleep.

> Thereunto does St. Paul exhort us, saying: "Put off concerning the former conversation the old man, which is corrupt according to the deceitful lusts; and be renewed in the spirit of your mind; and that ye put on the new man, which after God is created in righteousness and true holiness" (Ephesians 4:22, 24).

Just as children look like their parents, in the same way the children of this world (Luke 16:8) look like the world, worldly, and the children of God look like God, heavenly. It is a matter of inner disposition, of our inner face.

> Now he who lives to himself after the old man, is called and is truly a child of Adam; and though he may give diligence to the ordering of his life, he is still the child and brother of the Evil Spirit.

What an interesting statement: those who manifest the old man are both child and brother of Satan, the cosmic force of ignorance and evil. First we are born of Satan, and then as we begin to willingly act in a satanic manner we become a brother, a copy and coworker, of Satan. At first we are not responsible, but in time we come to be self-motivated and actively seeking out the ways of Satan. Then it can be said of us: "Ye are of your father the devil, and the lusts [desires] of your father ye will do" (John 8:44). We have become fully culpable for our actions and the will behind them.

> But he who lives in humble obedience and in the new man which is Christ, he is, in like manner, the brother of Christ and the child of God.

First we are God's child; then we are Christs as was Jesus; and finally we are gods.

> Behold! where the old man dies and the new man is born, there is that second birth of which Christ says, "Unless one is born again, he cannot see the kingdom of God" (John 3:3).

There is a place where the death of the old man and the birth of the new man occur. What is that place, and how is it found? It is the heart, the core, of our being, and we find it through the interior process of meditation, through yoga.

> Likewise St. Paul says, "As in Adam all die, even so in Christ shall all be made alive" (I Corinthians 15:22). That is to say, all who follow Adam in pride, in lust of the flesh, and in disobedience, are dead in soul, and never will or can be made alive but in Christ.

There is no cure for this state of spiritual death except awakening into our own Christhood. And there is no life outside Christ because that is our true nature. "So now also Christ shall be magnified in my body,.... For to me to live is Christ" (Philippians 1:20-21). This is not some artificial or assumed state, but our eternal Selfhood revealed.

> And for this cause, so long as a man is an Adam or his child, he is without God.

This is the plain fact and must be acknowledged. To think that because we adhere to a religion and "worship" or "profess" God in some manner we are not without God is a delusion. No matter how religious or pious we may seem to be, until we leave Adam behind and awaken and "put on Christ" (Galatians 3:27), the very form of Christ (Galatians 4:19) cannot be found in us, and we are not of Christ but of Adam and partakers in his death. Yet we can turn around (convert) and casting Adam aside become partakers of Christ and eventually Christs ourselves.

> **Christ says, "He that is not with me is against me" (Matthew 12:30). Now he who is against God, is dead before God. Whence it follows that all Adam's children are dead before God. But he who stands with Christ in perfect obedience, he is with God and lives. As it has been said already, sin lies in the turning away of the creature from the Creator, which agrees with what we have now said.**

This is pure truth that must be accepted and conformed to if we would ever rise into "newness of life" (Romans 6:4).

> **For he who is in disobedience is in sin, and sin can never be atoned for or healed but by returning to God, and this is brought to pass by humble obedience.**

We cannot just "confess" God and ascribe to some kind of religio-philosophical creed—we must return to God and become one with him as was Jesus. We, like him, must pray: "O Father, glorify thou me with thine own self with the glory which I had with thee before the world was" (John 17:5). Only by conforming ourselves to the divine life and pattern can we attain salvation: deliverance from the bonds and evils of this world.

The only "atonement for sin" is the attainment of holiness, of divine perfection. Neither Jesus nor we ourselves can atone for our sins by dying, but by living, by coming to life in our Christ-Self. "Even so in Christ shall all be made alive" (I Corinthians 15:22). We can have no other Savior but "Christ in you, the hope of glory" (Colossians 1:27).

THE OLD MAN AND THE NEW MAN

> For so long as a man continues in disobedience, his sin can never be blotted out; let him do what he will, it avails him nothing. Let us be assured of this. For disobedience is itself sin.
>
> But when a man enters into the obedience of the faith, all is healed, and blotted out and forgiven, and not else.

Once we quit pretending we are human and do all we can to reveal our divine nature, then our sins will be "blotted out and forgiven" and fade away like the fantasies they are. Then our true Self will be revealed to us.

"If even an evildoer worships me single-heartedly, he should be considered righteous, for truly he has rightly resolved. Quickly he becomes a virtuous soul and goes to everlasting peace. Understand: no devotee of me is ever lost.... Having come to this impermanent and unhappy world, devote yourself to me. With mind fixed on me, devoted, worshipping, bow down to me. Thus steadfast, with me as your supreme aim, you shall come to me" (Bhagavad Gita 9:30-31, 33-34).

> Insomuch that if the Evil Spirit himself could come into true obedience, he would become an angel again, and all his sin and wickedness would be healed and blotted out and forgiven at once. And could an angel fall into disobedience, he would straightway become an evil spirit although he did nothing afresh.

The ultimate salvation of all (*apokatastasis ton panton*) was a principle of original Christianity and is referred to by Saint Peter in Acts 3:21. There is no such thing as eternal damnation, because every sentient being is a part of God, and God certainly cannot be damned. And here the priest-knight tells us that Lucifer can be restored if he only wills to do so. And in time he will do so and be restored, as will all presently negative spirits.

The present state of evil or good is determined by which one we hold on to. The moment we let go and reach for the opposite condition we shall lay hold on it. Of course there will have to be a lot of learning and evolving before we are established in the positive state, but it will come about. What the author wants to get across to us is the fact that salvation and damnation are determined by our will, and nothing else. We decide which path we tread. Nothing will ever be automatic: throughout eternity we shall be with God because at every eternal moment we are willing to be so. And the "damned" will be alienated from God (though always with him, because that is his and their nature) because they will it to be so.

"One should uplift oneself by the lower self; one should not degrade oneself. The lower self can truly be a friend of the lower self, and the lower self alone can be an enemy of the lower self. For him who has conquered himself by the lower self, the lower self is a friend. But for him who has not conquered himself, the lower self remains hostile, like an enemy. The highest Self of him who has conquered himself and is peaceful, is thus steadfast in cold, heat, pleasure, pain, honor and dishonor" (Bhagavad Gita 6:5-7).

> If then it were possible for a man to renounce himself and all things, and to live as wholly and purely in true obedience, as Christ did in his human nature, such a man were quite without sin, and were one thing with Christ, and the same by grace which Christ was by nature.

Well, it *is* possible.

> But it is said this cannot be. So also it is said: "There is none without sin." But be that as it may, this much is certain; that the nearer we are to perfect obedience, the less we sin, and the farther from it we are, the more we sin.

The more we follow the law of dharma, inwardly and outwardly, the nearer we are to sinlessness.

> In brief: whether a man be good, better, or best of all; bad, worse, or worst of all; sinful or saved before God; it all lies in this matter of obedience.

It is a matter of the degree of conformity to the Divine. Exoteric theology is simply out of its depth when confronted by these things.

Therefore it has been said: the more of Self and Me, the more of sin and wickedness.

This is why Saint John the Baptist said: "He must increase, but I must decrease" (John 3:30).

So likewise it has been said: the more the Self, the I, the Me, the Mine, that is, self-seeking and selfishness, abate in a man, the more does God's I, that is, God himself, increase in him.

Here the Frankfurter tells us that the "I," the divine Self of God, is within the righteous man, and that "I" can increase until the righteous also can say: "I and my Father are one" (John 10:30).

Now, if all mankind abode in true obedience, there would be no grief nor sorrow. For if it were so, all men would be at one, and none would vex or harm another; so also, none would lead a life or do any deed contrary to God's will. Whence then should grief or sorrow arise? But now alas! all men, nay the whole world, lies in disobedience!

It will never happen that all the human race will be consciously united with God in this world, because this world is for those who are not one with God. As soon as we are one with God, we get what Ma Anandamayi called "a one-way ticket" out of here. As Sri Yukteswar told Yogananda: "Those who are too good for this world are adorning some other."

As I keep saying, it is a matter of one's own nature. That is why Krishna told Arjuna: "One acts according to one's own prakriti–even the wise man does so. Beings follow their own prakriti" (Bhagavad Gita 3:33). Prakriti determines the quality of our mind and action, and we determine the state of our prakriti by the orientation of our life, thoughts and deeds. "A man consists of his faith–he is what his faith is" (Bhagavad Gita 17:3). This is why yoga is the key to the transmutation of consciousness.

> Now were a man simply and wholly obedient as Christ was, all disobedience were to him a sharp and bitter pain. But though all men were against him, they could neither shake nor trouble him, for while in this obedience a man were one with God, and God himself were one with the man.

The highest form of obedience is conformity to love–love of God. Therefore the secret of such devotion and perfect unanimity with God is love. Love alone could bring about such consistent pushing aside of the world and such an adherence to God the way an oyster survives by the strength of its hold upon the rock.

There is no reasonable way to interpret the words about someone being one with God and God being one with that man except in an absolutely non-dual manner. In this book we find quite a bit of material on themes that can presuppose a duality between God and man, and then suddenly the Teutonic knight-priest slaps us in the face with a simple clause or two, usually in the last sentence, that impels us into recognition of the oneness that is attained by the faithful aspirant and which is imperative for all.

> Behold now all disobedience is contrary to God, and nothing else. In truth, no thing is contrary to God; no creature nor creature's work, nor anything that we can name or think of is contrary to God or displeasing to him, but only disobedience and the disobedient man.

God is all; therefore "no thing is contrary to God; no creature nor creature's work, nor anything that we can name or think of is contrary to God or displeasing to him" because all things are manifestations of God, formed of the light of the Holy Spirit and appearing at the will of God the Son (Ishwara). And the purpose of this appearance is the wooing of the wandering spirits to return to the Bosom of the Father.

As Yogananda said, there are only two kinds of human beings: the wise who seek God and the foolish who do not. Seeking is what the Frankfurter means by obedience, and not seeking is disobedience. It is very clear.

In short, all that is, is well-pleasing and good in God's eyes, saving only the disobedient man.

The disobedient may not be well-pleasing or good in God's eyes, but they are as much loved by him as the obedient—mostly because he knows that they all will in time become obedient and return to him.

But he is so displeasing and hateful to God and grieves him so sore, that if it were possible for human nature to die a hundred deaths, God would willingly allow them all for one disobedient man, that he might slay disobedience in him, and that obedience might be born again.

And he does. Because he is omnipresent and omniscient, God experiences every thing that all sentient beings in creation experience. He experiences the suffering and death as well as the happiness and life of even the smallest conscious being. It is not the disobedient that is "displeasing and hateful" to God, but the suffering and grief and continual death of the disobedient. "Those who are well have no need of a physician, but those who are sick. I did not come to call the righteous, but sinners" (Mark 2:17). The parables in the fifteenth chapter of Saint Luke of the Prodigal Son and the Shepherd seeking the one stray sheep depict the attitude of God toward the "sinner."

Behold! albeit no man may be so single and perfect in this obedience as Christ was, yet it is possible to every man to approach so near thereunto as to be rightly called Godlike, and "a partaker of the divine nature" (II Peter 1:4). And the nearer a man comes thereunto, and the more Godlike and divine he becomes, the more he hates all disobedience, sin, evil and unrighteousness, and the worse they grieve him.

How can we partake of the divine nature and not be "as Christ was"? What the righteous "hates" is the very thought of betraying God by ego and turning from God. He does not "hate the sin but not the sinner," because that too is a concession to ignorance. He loathes the very possibility of *his* falling away and forsaking God. He is not poking into other souls' follies and wanderings, but abhors the very possibility of himself betraying Christ and God with a kiss like Judas (Luke 22:48), as goes on every day throughout the religious world.

> Disobedience and sin are the same thing, for there is no sin but disobedience, and what is done of disobedience is all sin. Therefore all we have to do is to keep ourselves from disobedience.

We must keep in mind that our disobedience is to our own divine nature, not some abstract principles or "commandments." And how can that be even considered if love of God is not the beginning and the end of the quest? And how will we "keep ourselves from disobedience"? Through increasing awareness of the true God and our true Self. And that is possible through the inner path of yoga sadhana.

THE CHRIST LIFE

(CHAPTER EIGHTEEN)

**Of a truth we ought to know and believe that there is no life
so noble and good and well pleasing to God, as the life of Christ,
and yet it is to nature and selfishness the bitterest life.**

This is a sad truth. That which is the most wondrous and glorious, the Christ-life itself, is contrary to the illusion we call "nature" and is most bitter to the life of the selfish ego. "The natural man receiveth not the things of the Spirit of God: for they are foolishness unto him: neither can he know them, because they are spiritually discerned" (I Corinthians 2:14). This is one of the reasons they insist that no one can live as Jesus did. How terrible to see the children of God loathing and rejecting the highest life while reveling in the life of ego and evil like pigs in a sty. Frankly, this world has become a high-tech pig wallow of which the wallowing pigs love to boast.

It is grievous indeed that the sons of God, heirs to the kingdom of infinite consciousness and life, are following the way of the Prodigal Son who "would fain have filled his belly with the husks that the swine did eat" (Luke 15:16). Identity with their degraded life fills their minds. The "good things" of this world are nothing more than pig food, the "pigs" being the senses. So here we are, immortal spirits running after pig food, thinking we cannot live without it.

This conflict between the Christ life and that immersed in materiality is symbolized in the book of Revelation. "I went unto the angel, and said unto him, Give me the little book. And he said unto me, Take it, and eat it up; and it shall make thy belly bitter, but it shall be in thy mouth sweet as honey. And I took the little book out of the angel's hand, and ate it up;

and it was in my mouth sweet as honey: and as soon as I had eaten it, my belly was bitter." (Revelation 10:9-10).

Such is the contradiction between material and spiritual consciousness. Regarding this the Bhagavad Gita says: "That happiness which is like poison at first, but like amrita (that which makes one immortal) in the end, born of the light of one's own Self, is declared to be sattwic (see the glossary). That happiness arising from the contact of the senses with their objects, which in the beginning is like amrita but changes into that which is like poison, is declared to be rajasic [see the glossary]" (Bhagavad Gita 18:37-38).

A life of carelessness and freedom is to nature and the Self and the Me, the sweetest and pleasantest life, but it is not the best; and in some men may become the worst.

How anyone can miss the fact that people who live as they please (or rather, think they please) doing whatever they want (or think they want) and feeling no obligations or duties, end up absolutely miserable and desolate, is one of the wonders of being enmeshed in Maya. Even as a very small child I watched people and saw that at best their lives were uneventful boredom and at worst terrible sorrows and sufferings. I saw no one whose life was worth living, and as the years went by I realized that only those dedicated to the pursuit of spiritual life had purposeful and meaningful lives, that making God the center of all things was the only sensible way to live.

The Frankfurter divides life into the pleasant and the good; and so did the sages of India long before that, saying: "Different is the good, and different, indeed, is the pleasant. These two, with different purposes, bind a man. Of these two, it is well for him who takes hold of the good; but he who chooses the pleasant, fails of his aim. Both the good and the pleasant approach a man. The wise man, pondering over them, discriminates. The wise chooses the good in preference to the pleasant. The simple-minded, for the sake of worldly well-being, prefers the pleasant" (Katha Upanishad 1:2:1-2).

But though Christ's life be the most bitter of all, yet it is to be preferred above all.

Once a great medical genius, Dr. Josef Lenninger, went into the back of his office and came back with a cup of a clear yellow liquid. He told me to drink it and I did. "It tastes good," I commented. "Yes. Everything I have is good," he assured me, "but if you had any kind of liver trouble that would have tasted bitter to you. So from your reaction I know your liver is healthy." Sri Ramakrishna said that some liver disorders are cured by rock sugar (not the refined kind), but to those who have those disorders the sugar tastes bitter and they dislike it. In the same way, he said, those who are spiritually diseased find that which will help them distasteful and avoid it. But the wise force themselves to take those remedies and regain their health. The will is a major factor in spiritual life. "He that ruleth his spirit [is better] than he that taketh a city" (Proverbs 16:32).

Hereby shall you mark this: There is an inward sight which has power to perceive the One true Good, and that it is neither this nor that, but that of which St. Paul says; "When that which is perfect is come, then that which is in part shall be done away" (I Corinthians 13:10). By this he means, that the Whole and Perfect excels all the fragments, and that all which is in part and imperfect, is as nought compared to the Perfect.

This is very easy to understand, but of special note is the statement that God "is neither this nor that." Such is the teaching of the ancient seers of India. "Now therefore there is the teaching, Not This, Not This [Neti, Neti]" (Brihadaranyaka Upanishad 2.3.6). *A Brief Sanskrit Glossary* defines the process of Neti Neti as: "The way of describing the indescribable Brahman by enumerating what It is not; the analytical process of progressively negating all names and forms, in order to arrive at the eternal underlying Truth."

Nothing can be said about Brahman the Absolute and nothing can be said to be Brahman, for Brahman is the No-Thing, not an object of perception or description. On the other hand God is not Nothing because God is everything while still being No-Thing. Only the mind of the yogi can accurately comprehend this, because only the yogi possess the "inward sight which has power to perceive the One true Good": God.

> Thus likewise all knowledge of the parts is swallowed up when the Whole is known; and where that Good is known, it cannot but be longed for and loved so greatly, that all other love wherewith the man has loved himself and other things, fades away.

What a beautiful and equally accurate assessment of the situation for those who draw near and begin to see God, the Unseeable.

> And that inward sight likewise perceives what is best and noblest in all things, and loves it in the one true Good, and only for the sake of that true Good.

All things are seen to be in God and of God.

> Behold! where there is this inward sight, the man perceives of a truth, that Christ's life is the best and noblest life, and there-fore the most to be preferred, and he willingly accepts and en-dures it, without a question or a complaint, whether it please or offend nature or other men, whether he like or dislike it, find it sweet or bitter and the like.

This is true, but be assured that it will not be long before the aspirant will not *endure* the way of the Christ-life, but will *love* it next to God alone. He will not question or complain or be offended or dislike or find it bitter: to him it will be life itself. And he will be right. He will find the joyful truth of Jesus' assertion: "Come unto me, all ye that labour and are heavy laden, and I will give you rest. Take my yoke upon you, and learn of me; for I am meek and lowly in heart: and ye shall find rest unto your souls.

For my yoke is easy, and my burden is light" (Matthew 11:28-30). He will also heed the wondrous call: "If any man thirst, let him come unto me, and drink. He that believeth on me, as the scripture hath said, out of his belly shall flow rivers of living water" (John 7:37-38). He will understand fully the meaning of Saint Peter's words to Jesus: "To whom [else] shall we go? thou hast the words of eternal life" (John 6:68).

> And therefore wherever this Perfect and true Good is known, there also the life of Christ must be led, until the death of the body. And he who vainly thinks otherwise is deceived, and he who says otherwise, lies, and in what man the life of Christ is not, of him the true Good and eternal Truth will nevermore be known.

The prime question is this: How can you lead "the life of Christ" and not be Christ? It is impossible. Only those who have become Christs can lead that perfect holy life. Those who do not believe that each one must become a Christ–a Krishna, a Buddha, a Gorakhnath or a Sivananda–have not learned the first principle of authentic Christianity or any other genuine religion. But those who do so believe shall find in themselves the Christ, the hope of glory, and shall know God even as they are known by God (Colossians 1:27; I Corinthians 13:12). For they shall be One.

Entering the Christ-life

(Chapter Nineteen)

Let no one suppose, that we may attain to this true light and perfect knowledge, or life of Christ, by much questioning, or by hearsay, or by reading and study, nor yet by high skill and great learning.

Spiritual life cannot be derived from intellectual exercise. As the Frankfurter makes plain here, it cannot be found through mere intellectual inquiry, listening to discourses, study of books and any form of purely mental activity such as great skill in reason and argumentation or vast learning. That does not mean these things are not beneficial or desirable as long as we comprehend their limitations and do not mistake intellectual life for spiritual life. For none of these things lead to spiritual life.

But what is it we are supposed to seek? For the author is implying that these things are attainable. True light, perfect knowledge and the Christ-life are to be fervently sought after. Seeking these should not be considered useless or presumptuous. We must seek and obtain these three, for they are both the means and the fruits of spiritual life, of spiritual perfection. They are mystical in nature and transcend the ways of ordinary humanity.

Yes, so long as a man takes account of anything which is this or that, whether it be himself, or any other creature; or does anything, or frames a purpose, for the sake of his own likings or desires, or opinions, or ends, he comes not unto the life of Christ.

The perspective of those rightly seeking God is utterly different from that of ordinary people. We are to consider that all things are nothing that do not lead us onward in our spiritual quest. We must heed the reminder of Saint Paul: "Know ye not that your body is the temple of the Holy Ghost which is in you, which ye have of God, and ye are not your own? For ye are bought with a price: therefore glorify God in your body, and in your spirit, which are God's" (I Corinthians 6:19-20). "Ye are bought with a price; be not ye the servants of men.... let every man... abide with God" (I Corinthians 7:23-24).

> **This has Christ himself declared, for he says: "If any man will come after me, let him deny himself, and take up his cross, and follow me" (Matthew 16:24). "He that taketh not his cross, and followeth after me, is not worthy of me" (Matthew 10:38). And if he "hate not his father, and mother, and wife, and children, and brethren, and sisters, yea, and his own life also, he cannot be my disciple" (Luke 14:26). He means it thus: "He who does not forsake and part with everything, can never know My eternal truth, nor attain unto My life."**

This is simple truth, however much it is either shrugged off or actively opposed. We are to turn from everything but God. Those who lead "their" life and at the same time think they are going toward God are self-deluded.

An Eastern spiritual teacher once remarked to me that the problem with Westerners is their dividing up of their lives into compartments that run parallel with one another but do not affect one another. He said that Americans especially have "many hearts" rather than one which directs their entire life. So they create and dissolve as many compartments and hearts as they please. Forming a new compartment has no effect on the others at all. It is a spiritual form of schizophrenia, of multiple personality. Taking up a spiritual path has no effect on their total life, and dropping the path has no effect, either. In a sense their life is a bundle of unrelated whims. Rising or falling are fundamentally the same, since they really make no difference in the long run.

Sadly, the teacher was right. For half a century I have been observing the truth of his analysis. Long-standing friends who at one time seemed to be completely intent on God-realization have ended up totally materialistic and involved in (enslaved by) the world, seemingly unaware of the fact that they were going in a direction directly opposite to that which they had taken for years. I have seen people switch almost instantly from one mode of life to another directly opposed to the earlier one. Some have changed their religious orientation drastically, often instantly. It was as though they had never really believed anything, but just toyed with ideas which they tossed aside effortlessly and took up others that momentarily appealed to them. They did not have a divided heart, they had many separate hearts, as the teacher said. Saint James had such people in mind when he wrote: "A double minded man is unstable in all his ways.... Purify your hearts, ye double minded" (James 1:8; 4:8). This is why Saint Paul wrote: "Examine yourselves, whether ye be in the faith; prove [test] your own selves" (II Corinthians 13:5).

This is the reason that in every religion the monastic saints far outnumber the non-monastic saints. It is the nature of the world to be mixed and inconsistent, to be distracted by many currents of life and thought, to have many hearts. But the very nature of authentic monastic life is singleness of purpose and intent. And that is why non-monastics consider monastic life extreme and unnecessary, even mentally unhealthy, and never consider being monastic themselves. The single-mindedness the Frankfurter insists on is absolutely necessary for success in anything, and most especially in spiritual life. The inner life of the spirit and the outer life in the material world must be one, not two. If they are two, we can be confident that eventually the spiritual life will dissolve and only the material life will remain—and even be mistakenly considered spiritual.

Many are those seemingly spiritual people who follow the path of the fallen archangel regarding whom the prophet Isaiah said: "Hell from beneath is moved for thee to meet thee at thy coming: it stirreth up the dead for thee... All they shall speak and say unto thee, Art thou also become weak as we? art thou become like unto us? Thy pomp is brought down to the grave... and the worms cover thee. How art thou fallen from heaven,

O Lucifer, son of the morning! how art thou cut down to the ground,... For thou hast said in thine heart, I will ascend into heaven,... I will ascend above the heights of the clouds... Yet thou shalt be brought down to hell, to the sides of the pit. They that see thee shall narrowly look upon thee, and consider thee, saying,... thou art cast out of thy grave... trodden under feet... because thou hast destroyed thy land" (Isaiah 14:9-16, 19-20).

And though this had never been declared unto us, yet the truth herself says it, for it is so of a truth.

The priest-monk is referring to his previous sentence: "He means it thus: 'He who does not forsake and part with everything, can never know My eternal truth, nor attain unto My life.'" And note that here he equates truth with the Holy Spirit whom he refers to as "herself," the Divine Feminine.

It does not matter whether a person is formally monastic or not, total renunciation is an absolute necessity for those who will to become one with God. (Notice I say *will* not *wish*.) For it is impossible that we can embrace the All without first discarding the Nothing. Samsara must be left behind utterly before moksha (liberation) can be attained.

"Jesus entered into a certain village: and a certain woman named Martha received him into her house. And she had a sister called Mary, which also sat at Jesus' feet, and heard his word. But Martha was cumbered about much serving, and came to him, and said, Lord, dost thou not care that my sister hath left me to serve alone? bid her therefore that she help me. And Jesus answered and said unto her, Martha, Martha, thou art careful and troubled about many things: But one thing is needful: and Mary hath chosen that good part, which shall not be taken away from her" (Luke 10:38-42). The busybodying of Martha must cease and only the contemplation of Mary remain. It is not a matter of favoring one over the other, we must cast away the delusive aspects of the world and turn to God alone. Like Sister Gyanamata, Yogananda's greatest disciple, our motto must be "God First. God Alone."

Many people think that it is enough if God comes first in their lives, but God alone must *be* our life, for he is *Ekam Evam Advitiyam*—One Only

Without a Second. Our life must reflect God, so it, too, must be one only without a second. God has declared "there is none beside me" (Isaiah 45:6); therefore in our life there should be none beside God. What about "a balanced life"? Well, consider this: when a balance scale is perfectly balanced it reads Zero (0). I have met quite a few "balanced" yogis in the West, and I found very little yoga but a lot of talk–empty talk from an empty heart.

> **But so long as a man clings unto the elements and fragments of this world (and above all to himself), and holds converse with them, and makes great account of them, he is deceived and blinded, and perceives what is good no further than as it is most convenient and pleasant to himself and profitable to his own ends. These he holds to be the highest good and loves above all. Thus he never comes to the truth.**

The religious world is filled with people such as are described here. Those who hold to the world are self-deceived and self-blinded. All they will admit of religion and spirituality is that which is only "most convenient and pleasant to himself and profitable to his own ends." And God is never really their end and aim. This can especially be seen in the "householder yogis" that marry and divorce as often as they wish.

We must be like Saint Paul who said: "What things were gain to me, those I counted loss for Christ. Yea doubtless, and I count all things but loss for the excellency of the knowledge of Christ Jesus my Lord: for whom I have suffered the loss of all things, and do count them but dung, that I may win Christ, and be found in him, not having mine own righteousness,… but that which is… the righteousness which is of God" (Philippians 3:7-9).

The ability to distinguish between dung and divine righteousness is necessary. We must be sure we possess it. Then all will be well.

TURNING FROM THE REAL TO THE UNREAL

(CHAPTER TWENTY)

Now, since the life of Christ is every way most bitter to nature and the Self and the Me (for in the true life of Christ, the Self and the Me and nature must be forsaken and lost, and die altogether), therefore, in each of us, nature has a horror of it, and thinks it evil and unjust and a folly, and grasps after such a life as shall be most comfortable and pleasant to herself, and says, and believes also in her blindness, that such a life is the best possible.

It cannot be honestly denied that this paragraph describes the viewpoint of worldlings perfectly. There has been no era in history in which this was not true. The percentages of people so entrenched in material delusions may vary at different times, but the majority almost always hold this, perhaps not as an intellectual view but as an attitude. This is because such deluded people rarely speak openly, honestly and straightforwardly about their attitudes and thoughts on spiritual life.

They usually try to evade the subject, not because they are ashamed of their view, but because they are unsettled by talk on spiritual matters. So immersed are they in the world that the subject of the spiritual goes completely against the grain for them. Just as alcohol addicts truly do develop an aversion to water, so these people have an aversion to any subject that is not rooted in materiality and egotism–in anything that is not centered on them.

The truth that "in the true life of Christ, the Self and the Me and nature must be forsaken and lost, and die altogether" is not just bitter to them, but is considered deadly poison. However they may window-dress their objection to this fact that all which is not God must be cast out from us and our life-sphere for us to truly live is absolutely hateful to them. Their aversion may vary in degree and volubility regarding it, but outright hatred is at the heart of their aversion, so much so that dedication to God and the realization of God is loathed and upsets them when they encounter or observe it in others, even if it in no way affects or impinges upon their life. They cannot tolerate that which does not agree and conform to their adamant self-enslavement to the world and its ways. And this is true of exoteric religionists, as well.

As Saint James asked and stated: "Know ye not that the friendship of the world is enmity with God? whosoever therefore will be a friend of the world is the enemy of God" (James 4:4). His brother, Saint John, wrote: "Love not the world, neither the things that are in the world. If any man love the world, the love of the Father is not in him. For all that is in the world, the lust of the flesh, and the lust of the eyes, and the pride of life, is not of the Father, but is of the world. And the world passeth away, and the lust thereof: but he that doeth the will of God abideth for ever" (I John 2:15-17).

Jesus spoke more fully, saying: "If the world hate you, ye know that it hated me before it hated you. If ye were of the world, the world would love his own: but because ye are not of the world, but I have chosen you out of the world, therefore the world hateth you.... If I had not come and spoken unto them, they had not had sin: but now they have no cloke for their sin" (John 15:18-19, 22).

In the final sentence Jesus lays his finger on why they hate so virulently. I hope that in your education you did not encounter the kind of oafs that detest and complain about (and to) those that "ruin the grade curve" by applying themselves and doing well in their academic work. I did. They were the ones that on the first day of class asked the instructor: "Do you grade on the curve?" and would usually transfer out of the class if the teacher told them "No." They wanted something for nothing, a prime trait of those the Frankfurter is describing to us.

In spiritual life this type has the idea that if someone says their actions are wrong or lives a life that reveals theirs to be unworthy, then they are being condemned by them. Amazingly they think that if no one says or acts like something is wrong, then it is not wrong.

A very devout lady told me that her grandchildren were receiving no kind of religious instruction from their parents, so when they visited her for a few days she would talk to them about the principles of right and wrong. But after a few visits her granddaughter told her mother: "I don't want to go to grandma's house any more because she makes me have a black heart." Just think: She *makes* me have a black heart! Here we have the incorrigible delusion of the criminal: "The law makes me a crook." "I am in jail because the judge was against me."

One of my high school teachers grew up in the Saint Charles, Illinois, juvenile reformatory where his mother and father were "house parents." He told us that once after he was an adult and teaching public school, he visited his parents and saw that one boy there was only eight or nine years old. When he asked the boy why he was there, he answered in all seriousness: "I am here because I am too short." When he asked him how that could be, the boy told him that he had stolen a car, and because he was so short he could not see through the windshield and therefore ran the car into a tree, was caught and ended up in St. Charles–because he was too short.

I met a modern-day hermitess living outside Las Vegas, Nevada, in a cave. She was a most interesting and intelligent person. To explain her purpose would take too long here, but I want to tell you about an experience she had after a local newspaper had printed an article about her. One evening she saw a car drive up at the foot of the hill and a woman carrying a large revolver got out and came to stand in front of the cave, where she proceeded to fire six times at the hermitess, fortunately missing her each time. Then the woman threw down the gun, burst into tears and shouted at her: "Just look at what you made me do!" Then she went back down the hill, got in her car and drove away.

So the virtuous are disliked and even hated by the unvirtuous because by contrast they "make" them "bad." In response to virtue such a person "has a horror of it, and thinks it evil and unjust and a folly,"

Now, nothing is so comfortable and pleasant to nature, as a free, careless way of life, therefore she clings to that, and takes enjoyment in herself and her own powers, and looks only to her own peace and comfort and the like.

The rationalizations of such people for their way of life can be really astonishing, including those of the "balanced yogis" I mentioned previously. Especially amazing are their rationalizations for not leading the monastic life.

And this happens most of all, where there are high natural gifts of reason, for that soars upwards in its own light and by its own power, till at last it comes to think itself the true Eternal Light, and gives itself out as such, and is thus deceived in itself, and deceives other people along with it, who know no better, and also are thereunto inclined.

Some people really are too smart for their own good, because they can so cleverly convince themselves and others that there is no need to overdo things and become a religious fanatic and lead an abnormal life. The parable of the fox without a tail almost always applies to them.

Honest to God

(Chapter Twenty One)

Now, it may be asked, what is the state of a man who follows the true Light to the utmost of his power? I answer truly, it will never be declared aright, for he who is not such a man, can neither understand nor know it, and he who is, knows it indeed; but he cannot utter it, for it is unspeakable.

This paragraph could easily have come from a yogic or philosophical text of India, and shows that truth is universal, that those who draw near enough to God will speak the same thing whatever their religious tradition might be.

For example, the hermitess Juliana of Norwich was told by Jesus (a voice from a crucifix) that all mankind will ultimately attain salvation. Nothing could have been more opposed to the everlasting damnation teaching of the Western Christian Church at that time. It was assumed that the majority of humanity would go to hell forever at their death. Both theological and liturgical texts affirmed this over and over. Yet Juliana learned from Jesus himself that it was not the truth.

Many Christian saints have spoken and acted contrary to the official teachings of the Church. For example, Padre Pio (Saint Pio of Pietrelcina) gave communion to my friend Steven Wyland who was Jewish, not Catholic, and told him he would be his spiritual father. At another time when he was told that one of his spiritual children believed in reincarnation, he replied: "It makes no difference what someone believes about reincarnation. What matters is whether they are trying to find God now." Once a man went to confession and told Padre Pio that he practiced yoga meditation. "Keep it up," Padre Pio said, "it is a good thing."

Teresa Neuman the stigmatist told one of Yogananda's disciples that a Catholic was anyone whose heart was open to God, and those who belonged to the Catholic Church but whose hearts were closed to God were not Catholics. "And you are a Catholic," she insisted, even though he had been raised a Protestant and had become a yogi and a sannyasi.

Saint John of Kronstadt, a Russian Orthodox saint, on occasion prayed with Moslems even though the Eastern Orthodox Church rules say that if anyone prays with someone who is not Orthodox, if they are a priest they are automatically suspended and if a layman they are excommunicated. The instances in which saints have gone completely against the party line are innumerable.

The main thrust of this paragraph, though, is the important fact that no one can conceive of the spiritual condition of an enlightened person. It is truly sad to see ignoramuses running around investigating and challenging contemporary yogis as to whether they are enlightened or not. Some of their "tests" are as ridiculous as they are ignorant.

The monk-priest tells us that an unenlightened person cannot possibly understand or know the experience of the enlightened, and the enlightened cannot explain or adequately describe it because it is beyond all thought and speech.

It is most beneficial that the Bhagavad Gita be read daily by the yogi, because there the state of liberation is described as much as can be, and what is described can only be known by the liberated one because it is totally internal and of a character that cannot be observed by others. Plenty of people try to act enlightened, but the Gita tells the truth of the matter: the enlightened of necessity remain silent on the subject and the unenlightened should remain silent, too, as nothing they can say will be true since they really know nothing of it. Daily reading of the Gita is the best safeguard against delusion and mistaken conclusions.

Therefore let him who would know it, give his whole diligence that he may enter therein; then will he see and find what has never been uttered by man's lips.

Self/God realization can only be known by diligent practice. Therefore the wise keeps his attention on his sadhana and has little, if anything, to say to those who are not also dedicated to spiritual practice. For it is practice alone that makes perfect, not words or holy show. "He whose happiness is within, whose delight is within, whose illumination is within: that yogi, identical in being with Brahman, attains Brahmanirvana" (Bhagavad Gita 5:24).

> However, I believe that such a man has liberty as to his outward walk and conversation, so long as they consist with what must be or ought to be; but they may not consist with what he merely wills to be.

A large number of spiritual rogues and dacoits have been excused in the eyes of others by the propagation of the "crazy wisdom" rationalization by which demonic behavior is declared to be angelic (even divine) when the monster is supposedly enlightened and beyond it all. But the Frankfurter rightly says that an enlightened person acts in absolute consonance with his perfect inner state at all times. If he acts according to private whim in a manner inconsistent with righteousness and good sense, then he is not enlightened at all.

How I wish you could have spent time with Swami Sivananda. He was a supreme yogi, a god walking the earth, and at the same time thoroughly sensible and impeccable in his speech and action.

> But oftentimes a man makes to himself many must-be's and ought-to-be's which are false.

It took quite a number of years, but finally when I was twenty I figured out that in religion many people choose what they want to believe and then look through the scriptures to see what supports their ideas and then go shopping for a group that teaches those ideas. Many more really never spend their time thinking about religion at all, but just find a group where they like the décor or the convenience of location or feel at home or feel wanted or even needed, and join it. The reasons could be either important or trivial, but in both instances it was choice on the part of the individual.

In most people ego is the seeker and finder, yet in some the spirit-Self is seeking or is being sought by God. This is a different situation altogether.

So the question must always be applied: Is this the will of the individual or an intuiting and response to the will of God? Who ultimately is the mover in this situation? This is a serious matter and its importance cannot be over-estimated.

> **The which you may see hereby, that when a man is moved by his pride or covetousness or other evil dispositions, to do or leave undone anything, he ofttimes says, "It must needs be so, and ought to be so."**
>
> **Or if he is driven to, or held back from anything by the desire to find favor in men's eyes, or by love, friendship, enmity, or the lusts and appetites of his body, he says, "It must needs be so, and ought to be so." Yet behold, that is utterly false.**

Of course a lot of people do what they want and claim that it is God's will. And in a sense it is, because their ego is their god, not the true God. People are always being "guided" to do what is supposedly the divine will, but divinity usually proves to be a very poor judge and guide. I knew a man who married a very obvious looney "because God told me to." But God did not foot the bill for the divorce he filed for six months later. The number of people now being directed by "angels" and "guides" is increasing daily. But there, too, the angels and guides prove to be very fickle and worthless. Yet I have never known a single one of that type who would admit that it was just their whim and that their "guidance" had came from their own egoic mind.

Of course the plain old "I have to do this" still is found everywhere. I knew a woman who "knew" she was to marry Sylvester Stallone. It was her destiny and was part of the cosmic plan. She would go to psychics, diviners and astrologers and ask them what they saw for her future. Of course, not one of them ever told her she was to marry Sylvester Stallone, so she would fly into a rage and denounce them as frauds and fools. She would even on occasion find out where Stallone would be and tell everyone that she was going meet him at last and become his wife. She would go there and not say a word to him, but would come back and keep going on about her destiny to marry him.

Every person that has told me they have "been driven" to do something has proved to be fooled by their own tangled mind and nothing ever came of it but confusion, of which they had plenty before.

I am confident that all this has been going on for as long as the human race has existed.

> Had we no must-be's, nor ought-to-be's, but such as God and the Truth show us, and constrain us to, we should have less, forsooth, to order and do than now; for we make to ourselves much disquietude and difficulty which we might well be spared and raised above.

If we will stop all whimsical doings and forcibly examine our minds and through spiritual cultivation learn what is and is not in the divine will for us, our lives will become very simple and clear. Not that no difficulties at all will arise, because that is the nature of earthly life. But we will live in peace and safety. Most of the holy ones I have known lived quietly, even secretly, invisible to the world at large. If we follow their example we will become like them: transformed from unreal to real; from darkness to light; from death to immortality.

The Spirit of Satan and the Spirit of God

(Chapter Twenty Two)

Before I can comment on this chapter I want to give you some background information about evil and evil spirits—a subject we must take into consideration so we can understand the author's words.

Satan—the Outer Darkness

There is a force of cosmic evil. It is not a person, but a vast and powerful aggregation of negative energies and energy patterns. It possesses a magnetism that draws to itself wandering bands or bundles of negative energies. And since everything is inherently intelligent, being formed of the light and power of the Holy Spirit, it can even manifest a kind of robotic intelligence and will. Furthermore, it attracts to itself and swallows up wandering intelligences that have an affinity with its negative power and mode of existence. Think of it as a mobile hell consisting of negative energies and individual negative intelligences.

There was a time on earth when slave traders wandered around with their prisoners, selling and buying human beings. In the same way this force roves through the creation dispensing and absorbing negativity and negative intelligences. It is the Outer Darkness spoken of by Jesus (Matthew 8:12), a prison consisting of both energies and intelligences all bound up with one another. As I say, it is a kind of hell, and its inhabitants are a kind of demon. Some have virtually no power but are slaves driven by its energies, others are sentient beings that are both workers and slaves and others are extremely powerful beings of great intelligence, strength and malevolence. These latter are fallen archangels and beings similar to them. The totality

124

of this boiling and roiling conglomerate is "Satan" or "the Devil."

Outer Darkness in the Gospel of Matthew is *exoteros skotos*. We get the word exoteric, outwardly turned or oriented, from *exoteros*. It indicates that which is totally material in manifestation and orientation. The energies of the Outer Darkness produce external consciousness in whatever they touch, and the intelligences in the Outer Darkness have absolutely no inner awareness whatsoever; they are literally "soulless" in the sense that they have no idea whatsoever of their true nature as spirits. This is why many of those under their influence are materialists and deny both the psychic and the spiritual levels of existence. They themselves are virtual embodiments of that delusion. They are outside–alienated from–all reality, including the Supreme Reality: God.

Skotos is not just absence of physical light, but mental blindness or ignorance. *Strong's Concordance* has this definition: "Ignorance respecting divine things and human duties, and the accompanying ungodliness and immorality, together with their consequent misery; persons in whom darkness becomes visible and holds sway." The sixteenth chapter of the Bhagavad Gita is devoted to a consideration of the divine and demonic personalities. At death these latter usually "go to hell" but the worst of them become part of the Outer Darkness from which there is no escape until the creation is dissolved at the end of the present creation cycle. This is the hell of hells, the darkness of the dark.

Skotos comes from *skia*, from which we get our word sketch. *Skotos* is the state which blocks all light, all truth or right perception. It is also a shadow that appears to be real, a form that is only an appearance and not the object it seems to be. *Skotos* is always insubstantial, essentially an illusion, therefore a lie. It can also mean a purely minimal thing or being, like a husk or shell. Perhaps the best simile is that of an object that has been burnt and retains its original shape, but when touched breaks or falls into mere ashes. Thus the Outer Darkness is also the Maya of maya.

This is an ugly subject, but one that needs to be understood. The usual concept of Satan is completely wrong, and needs to be differentiated from ordinary negative energies and entities that are bad enough. However they can be neutralized or banished by human beings without much effort.

Should we fear Satan? No; we should only fear that which would bring us into affinity with it and enable it to influence and even assimilate us. Those who pursue positive thought and deed need never concern themselves with Satan, for their positive vibrations will keep it far from them.

Obsession and Possession

There are two modes of interference of negative spirits: obsession and possession.

Obsession is when the entity is attached to the aura and influences the person, who is aware of intense pressure to do or say something. (Do you know someone who habitually says: "I don't know why I'm doing this…" or "I don't know where this is coming from…"?) If the obsessed person's will is strong it is merely an unpleasant urge; if the will is weak the person speaks or acts, sometimes against his will, feeling that he is being forced to do what he does not really want to do.

The obsessing entity can sometimes penetrate into the person's body and cause various sensations and physical conditions. For example, I met a man who was suffering from terrible headaches because an entity had entered and was affecting a center in his brain. When that area on the outside of his head was touched and a mantra silently intoned, the entity instantly left along with the headaches. Obsession is much more common than possession.

Possession is when an entity enters the body and takes over its functions to some degree or even totally. This is rarer than obsession, because we guided the growth of our bodies in the womb and it is specifically ours, an instrument of our personal karma. Therefore it is difficult for another consciousness to control it. Often the possessed person seems to be deeply impaired, the body becoming paralyzed or distorted in some manner because the entity cannot fully take it over. Some possessed people become blind or mute.

There are five kinds of possession. 1) The person watches from within as his body moves and acts seemingly on its own without his willing it. 2) The person is pushed out of his body into his aura and watches its action. 3) The person is pushed completely out of his aura and watches from a distance or goes wandering off somewhere, but remains connected. In these first three conditions the possessed may hear the possessing entity speaking to him. 4) The person blacks out and has no experience or memory of anything that takes place during the possession. 5) The person is expelled from his body and becomes a wandering spirit as the entity possesses the body completely. Such a person is for all purposes actually dead.

According to Dr. Benoytosh Bhattacharya, the father of modern radionics and a great yogi, there are two symptoms of possession: 1) a perpetual and regular skipping of one to three heartbeats, and 2) absence of a heartbeat altogether and in its place a kind of heavy current or vibration in the veins and chest. In the first instance the person is possessed and being completely controlled. In the second one, the person is dead and the entity has taken over totally. But please be aware that simple arrhythmia of the heartbeat should not be mistaken for a symptom of possession. In possession it is something more irregular and constant.

Lesser negative energies and intelligences can indeed be encountered by us, but those who keep their minds fixed on God will find they are safe. In the Gospels and the lives of saints we find that evil spirits often declare that they are being "burned" or in some other way tormented by the presence of a holy person or object. Therefore if remembrance of him who is the Holy God, Holy Mighty and Holy Immortal is strong within us they will stay away from us. My paternal grandmother and one of her sisters would stop all negative psychic activity just by being in the room. I witnessed this myself.

Now for the Frankfurter's words.

> **It is written that sometimes the Devil and his spirit do so enter into and possess a man, that he knows not what he does and leaves undone, and has no power over himself, but the Evil Spirit has the mastery over him, and does and leaves undone in, and with, and through, and by the man what he will.**

This is a description of both obsession and possession. Unevolved or weak-minded people can be totally controlled through obsession. Even more, those who have been negatively polarized through lifetimes of wrong action can be so conditioned that they simply do not have the ability to consider their situation objectively. So they go through life like robots or puppets, never considering or questioning their thoughts or deeds, somewhat like sleepwalkers.

Many people are in this state without being actually obsessed or possessed. Negativity has become second nature to them. But whichever it might be, the individual must become freed from all evil influences. Oftentimes this can be done by another person such as an exorcist or someone with psychic and spiritual powers and the knowledge of how to free others. It can be very easy, difficult or even impossible. Sometimes this condition comes as a result of negative karmas. In such a case the person must fulfill a karmic sentence. Then one day the cloud will lift and they will be free.

Free will is a result of spiritual evolution. Most people have free whimsy, willing bondage and willful enslavement.

It is true in a sense that all the world is subject to and possessed with the Evil Spirit, that is, with lies, falsehood, and other vices and evil ways; this also comes of the Evil Spirit, but in a different sense.

There is no doubt that this world is a negative and spiritually polluted environment. Ever since the Luciferic rebellion numberless spirits have been striving to distort every aspect of earth life. Death itself is a product of those evil intelligences, as is all wrong thought, deed and corrupted nature. Since the spirit is ever free and untouched by any evil, eventually all will shed the bonds of negativity and begin their return to God, rising into the unfailing Light. So we need not be pessimistic about the ultimate fate of all sentient beings. Their salvation is assured. What we need to do is get concerned about our own present and future and do our best to turn ourselves around one hundred and eighty degrees and travel the path to the Divine.

> Now, a man who should be in like manner possessed by the Spirit of God, so that he should not know what he does or leaves undone, and have no power over himself, but the will and Spirit of God should have the mastery over him, and work, and do, and leave undone with him and by him, what and as God would; such a man were one of those of whom St. Paul says: "For as many as are led by the Spirit of God, they are the sons of God" (Romans 8:14), and they "are not under the law, but under grace" (Romans 6:14), and to whom Christ says: "For it is not ye that speak, but the Spirit of your Father which speaketh in you" (Matthew 10:20).

Here there may be a problem in translation since God does not obsess or possess as evil spirits do. In fact, one sign of evil influence is its coercive character, its subversion of the individual's will. Clearly we are told in the Bible that "the spirits of the prophets are subject to the prophets" (I Corinthians 14:32), they are not possessed "vehicles" of spirit overshadowing. Passivity has no place in spiritual life. Even inaction should be an act of will, not slack-mouthed surrender.

The great masters tell us that there is a state in which a person automatically does what is right as a manifestation of his awakened consciousness. Such a one has gone beyond good and evil in the sense that he no longer does something because it is considered good or abstains from something because it is considered evil. Rather, he does good because he is good, and does not do evil because he is not evil. It is totally a matter of his internal state. Ego has died and so has ignorance; therefore he lives in this world with God consciousness, aware of his divine Self. Every aspect of his life is pervaded by this awareness which is his true nature.

Jesus indicates this when he says: "Beware of false prophets, which come to you in sheep's clothing, but inwardly they are ravening wolves. Ye shall know them by their fruits. Do men gather grapes of thorns, or figs of thistles? Even so every good tree bringeth forth good fruit; but a corrupt tree bringeth forth evil fruit. A good tree cannot bring forth evil fruit, neither can a corrupt tree bring forth good fruit.... Wherefore by their fruits ye shall know them" (Matthew 7:15-18, 20). Earlier I cited the Bhagavad Gita: "One acts according to one's own prakriti–even the wise man does so. Beings follow their own prakriti; what will restraint accomplish?" (Bhagavad Gita 3:33).

Swami Sivananda coined the motto: "Be good. Do good." First we *become* good, become our true Self, and then spontaneously we will *do* good. There is really no other way to do true good. Then God will act through us because we are a part of God.

Jesus expressed it this way: "Verily, verily, I say unto you, The Son can do nothing of himself, but what he seeth the Father do: for what things soever he doeth, these also doeth the Son likewise" (John 5:19). "I do nothing of myself; but as my Father hath taught me, I speak these things" (John 8:28). And lest we use the excuse that Jesus was unique (an excuse I heard a lot when I was a Protestant), he assures us: "Verily, verily, I say unto you, He that believeth on me, the works that I do shall he do also; and greater works than these shall he do; because I go unto my Father" (John 14:12). All we need do is to "go unto the Father" as did he.

> But I fear that for one who is truly possessed with the Spirit of God, there are a hundred thousand or an innumerable multitude possessed with the Evil Spirit. This is because men have more likeness to the Evil Spirit than to God. For the Self, the I, the Me and the like, all belong to the Evil Spirit, and therefore it is, that he is an Evil Spirit. Behold one or two words can utter all that has been said by these many words: "Be simply and wholly bereft of Self." But by these many words, the matter has been more fully sifted, proved, and set forth.

It is a matter of will: we either choose to follow the ego and its ways or we choose to follow our spirit-Self. We alone choose and carry out our choice. "Work out your own salvation with fear and trembling. For it is God which worketh in you both to will and to do of his good pleasure" (Philippians 2:12-13). Every one of us needs to reach the realization: "I and my Father are one" (John 10:30).

Now men say, "I am in no wise prepared for this work, and therefore it cannot be wrought in me," and thus they find an excuse, so that they neither are ready nor in the way to be so.

All along the way I have heard: "I am not ready" from the spiritual lay-abouts. "I'm not like you;" "I'm not advanced enough;" "It will take more lives before I can do that." But the priest-knight tells the truth when he says:

And truly there is no one to blame for this but themselves. For if a man were looking and striving after nothing but to find a preparation in all things, and diligently gave his whole mind to see how he might become prepared; verily God would well prepare him, for God gives as much care and earnestness and love to the preparing of a man, as to the pouring in of his Spirit when the man is prepared.

The moment we decide to enter the way of life eternal, God and his angels and saints come to our aid–if we really want it. Otherwise they leave us alone, for wasting time is a form of dishonesty in which they never engage. People may not want to take responsibility for their spiritual laziness, but it is theirs anyway, and we should "respect" that and leave them alone.

Once a man said to Yogananda: "My habit is so strong; how can I change without your blessing?" And Yogananda told him: "Well, my blessing is there. God's blessing is there. Only your blessing is needed!"

Yet there be certain means thereunto, as the saying is, "To learn an art which you know not, four things are needful."

Now we are going to discover what we need to make lasting spiritual progress.

The first and most needful of all is, a great desire and diligence and constant endeavor to learn the art. And where this is wanting, the art will never be learned.

Finding God must be the central endeavor of our life. Everything else must be secondary. That is why Jesus said: "Seek ye first the kingdom of God" (Matthew 6:33). He who offers God second place offers him no place. Without "great desire and diligence and constant endeavor" no one finds God. And as the Frankfurter assures us, where that is lacking nothing will be attained.

The second is, a copy or example by which you mayest learn.

The lives of saints and masters should be read by us so we can see how success in spiritual life is gained, and how it is not gained. We must both do what they did and avoid what they avoided. Especially we need to study the lives of great yogis and follow their example.

The third is to give earnest heed to the master, and watch how he works, and to be obedient to him in all things, and to trust him and follow him.

Masters are not easy to find, so often we will have to study the written teachings of great masters such as Krishna, Buddha, Jesus and others. The Bhagavad Gita should be central to our spiritual study and should be read every day of our lives. Many of the aspiring yogis of East and West who failed would not have done so if they had made the teachings and perspective of the Gita their own. Otherwise life becomes like walking blindfolded through a mine field.

The fourth is to put your own hand to the work, and practice it with all industry.

We must put forth effort, diligent effort, and sustained effort. That is why the yogis in India say: *Banat, banat, banjai!* (Making, making made! or Doing, doing, done!) I once read a book by a Buddhist monk who said three things were needed for spiritual success: Perseverance, Perseverance, Perseverance. Swami Sivananda actually used to sing: "D. I. N.; D. I.

N.; D. I. N.; Do It Now; Do It Now; Do It Now." "Behold, now is the accepted time; behold, now is the day of salvation" (II Corinthians 6:2), said Saint Paul. We have no other time but Now.

> But where one of these four is wanting, the art will never be learned and mastered. So likewise is it with this preparation. For he who has the first, that is, thorough diligence and constant, persevering desire towards his end, will also seek and find all that appertains thereunto, or is serviceable and profitable to it. But he who has not that earnestness and diligence, love and desire, seeks not, and therefore finds not, and therefore remains ever unprepared. And therefore he never attains unto that end.

It is our neglect and disregard that eventually forces God to say: "How often would I have gathered thy children together, even as a hen gathereth her chickens under her wings, and ye would not! Behold, your house is left unto you desolate" (Matthew 23:37-38).

THE WAY TO PEACE

(CHAPTER TWENTY THREE)

There are some who talk of other ways and preparations to this end, and say we must lie still under God's hand, and be obedient and resigned and submit to him. This is true; for all this would be perfected in a man who should attain to the uttermost that can be reached in this present time. But if a man ought and is willing to lie still under God's hand, he must and ought also to be still under all things, whether they come from God himself, or the creatures, nothing excepted. And he who would be obedient, resigned and submissive to God, must and ought to be also resigned, obedient and submissive to all things, in a spirit of yielding, and not of resistance, and take them in silence, resting on the hidden foundations of his soul, and having a secret inward patience, that enables him to take all chances or crosses willingly, and whatever befalls, neither to call for nor desire any redress, or deliverance, or resistance, or revenge, but always in a loving, sincere humility to cry, "Father, forgive them, for they know not what they do!"

The ordinary Christian view of this subject is passive masochism: submit to "the suffering" of "the cross" and expiate your sins and even the sins of others. The "shut up and suffer" doctrine is not just mistaken, it is morally insane. And that insanity is based on ignorance: ignorance of the three fundamental facts of human existence. They are: 1) karma, 2) reincarnation; 3) evolution of consciousness. We should analyze these words of the Frankfurter in the perspective of these three principles, since the Inquisition is no longer around to torture and kill us for knowing the truth of things.

In the Genesis account of creation we are told seven times that God "saw that it was good." The word *ra'ah* means to consider. The idea is that God considered his creation to be good. *Towb* means good, pleasing, beautiful, precious, beneficial and even joyful. It is much more than just all right. Why? Because it is the means by which humanity can reach divinity through mastery of external and internal being. (See *Robe of Light.*) It is the mechanism, the ladder, by which sentient beings can ascend in consciousness and power. That is why the Creed found in the fourth edition of *The Liberal Catholic Liturgy* says: "We believe in the law of good which rules the world, and by which one day all His sons shall reach the feet of the Father, however far they stray." Creation and salvation (liberation/perfection) are inseparable. But those who do not follow the laws inherent in the creation for their ascension in consciousness will find themselves whirled around, confused and tossed into suffering and great fear, the *mahato bhayat* Krishna speaks of in the Bhagavad Gita (2:40).

The attitudes the author speaks of are usually misinterpreted as a kind of passive "take whatever comes" outlook which is little more than "shut up and don't draw attention to yourself," a policy that certainly did help in the Nazi concentration camps. But God's creation is certainly not a concentration camp and he is no Nazi commandant. The idea that all our troubles are just God kicking us around for our own good and that it is virtuous to smile through our tears and say: "Thank you, Sir, may I have another?" is morally insane and blasphemous.

All the trouble and misery of the world is created by those who live in a manner inconsistent with the divine plan for their betterment. And by that I do not mean that when we go against God's laws we get punished–a kind of reversal of the lab rats getting rewards for running mazes correctly. If we put our finger in a flame it will be burnt and great pain will result. It is not punishment from God, but the natural consequence. A religion that divides everything into reward and punishment, happiness for the obedient and pain for the disobedient, is creating a mental concentration camp for its adherents. And, as Jesus said: "According to your faith be it unto you" (Matthew 9:29). In false religion God is continually blamed for the results of our own wrong thinking. It makes a vast difference when we openly believe and affirm the assurance of Saint Paul: "Ye are all the children of light, and the children of the day: we are not of the night, nor of darkness" (I Thessalonians 5:5). We become freed from the shadowland of negativity and ignorance.

Swami Sriyukteswar Giri, the guru of Paramhansa Yogananda, sang a song which sets forth the right way to deal with negativity: "Desire, my great enemy, with his soldiers surrounding me, is giving me lots of trouble.... That enemy I will defeat, remaining in the castle of peace." If we follow this wisdom then it can be said of us: "He acts untainted by evil as a lotus leaf is not wetted by water" (Bhagavad Gita 5:7-10). If we fix our mind on God and on the things of the spirit, truly purifying ourselves in a positive way, walking in light and not in darkness, then we will live at peace and in happy fulfillment.

Frankly, people who are obsessed with the negative and the evil, and especially "the Devil" and demons, have an affinity for such things and like to think about them. "For where your treasure is, there will your heart be also" (Matthew 6:21).

Here is a poem I heard when I was just a child that says it quite well.

> Once on the edge of a quiet pool,
> Under the bank where 'twas nice and cool,
> Just where the stream flowed out of the bay,
> There sat a grumpy and mean old frog,
> Who sat all day in the sand to soak,
> And just did nothing but croak and croak.
> A blackbird hollered, "I say, you know,
> What is the matter down there below?
> Are you in trouble or pain or what?"
> The old frog growled, "Mine is an awful lot."
> "'Tis a dirty world," thus the old frog spoke—
> "Croakety, croakety, croakety, croak."
> Then the blackbird said. "I see what's wrong.
> Why don't you smile or sing a song?
> Look up, young feller, why bless my soul,

You're looking down a muskrat hole!"
A wise old turtle, who boarded near,
Said to the blackbird, "Now, friend, see here,
Don't waste no tears on him," says he.
"That fool's down there, 'cause he wants to be."

My Aunt Faye who read it to me then said: "You have to decide if you will look up to God or down to earth; up to heaven or down to hell."

Behold! this is a good path to that which is Best, and a noble and blessed preparation for the farthest goal which a man may reach in this present time. This is the lovely life of Christ, for he walked in the aforesaid paths perfectly and wholly unto the end of his bodily life on earth. Therefore there is no other and better way or preparation to the joyful life of Jesus Christ, than this same course, and to exercise oneself therein, as much as may be. And of what belongs thereunto we have already said somewhat; nay, all that we have here or elsewhere said and written, is but a way or means to that end.

To simply live life continually elevating our consciousness, yoked to yoga, will take care of everything. Living on earth we can keep our minds in heaven, not through mere positive thinking but through the positive state of being that is produced through yoga. For that is our true being which is always present. We need only place our consciousness within it and we have gone to heaven. Instead of battling and resisting evil, we immerse ourself in the divine good that is our eternal Self. As Emily Dickinson wrote: "Instead of getting to heaven at last, I'm going all along!" The way of Christ is total absorption in God. As Yogananda said in one of his talks about his life: "My two eyes were on God." May it be so with us.

But what the end is, knows no man to declare. But let him who would know it, follow my counsel and take the right path thereunto, which is the humble life of Jesus Christ; let him

strive after that with unwearied perseverance, and so, without doubt, he shall come to that end which endures for ever. "He that endureth to the end shall be saved" (Matthew 10:22).

A lot of ignorant people are humble. What is needed is to be dedicated to God, to fill our awareness with God. "Simple piety" is a myth. Truly spiritual people are not simple in the least. Their minds are awakened and evolved so they follow the divine path wisely and rightly. Satan (delusion) never fools them.

Certainly those who persevere to the end are saved, because God and God alone is the End, the Goal.

The Gita speaks

Here is what the Bhagavad Gita has to say about the person who lives life aright and therefore comes to live in God.

"When he leaves behind all the desires of the mind, contented in the Self by the Self, then he is said to be steady in wisdom. He whose mind is not agitated in misfortunes, freed from desire for pleasures, from whom passion, fear and anger have departed, steady in thought—such a man is said to be a sage. He who is without desire in all situations, encountering this or that, pleasant or unpleasant, not rejoicing or disliking—his wisdom stands firm. And when he withdraws completely the senses from the objects of the senses, as the tortoise draws in its limbs, his wisdom is established firmly. Sense-objects turn away from the abstinent, yet the taste for them remains. But the taste also turns away from him who has seen the Supreme. The troubling senses forcibly carry away the mind of even the striving man of wisdom. Restraining all these senses, he should sit in yoga, intent on me. Surely, he whose senses are controlled—his consciousness stands steadfast and firm. This is the divine state. Having attained this, he is not deluded. Fixed in it even at the time of death, he attains Brahmanirvana" (Bhagavad Gita 2:55-61, 72).

CHRIST: THE UNION OF GOD AND MAN

(CHAPTER TWENTY FOUR)

Moreover there are yet other ways to the lovely life of Christ, besides those we have spoken of: to wit, that God and man should be wholly united, so that it can be said of a truth, that God and man are one.

Jesus' statement: "I and my Father are one" (John 10:30), is acceptable to exoteric Christianity if it is confined to Jesus, but not in the intended sense that all human beings can and will be one with God just as Jesus was. Exoteric Christianity insists that Jesus was unique, that no one can be what he was. Yet, Jesus not only said: "*I* am the light of the world" (John 8:12), he also said to his disciples: "*Ye* are the light of the world" (Matthew 5:14). And: "Verily, verily, I say unto you, He that believeth on me, *the works that I do shall he do also; and greater works than these shall he do*" (John 14:12). How can this be? Because in essence God and man are eternally one. All sentient beings are verily rooted in God the Ground and the Source of their being as well as their Goal. Human beings are intended to be Christs, which is what "Christian" means: Other Christs. So if this truth is not taught and believed it is not Christianity.

The hysterical resistance to this understanding is because it then has to be admitted that we are not only capable of being what Jesus is, we are obligated to do our best to realize that potential. People would much rather be "sinners saved by grace" than saints who toughed it out and made it through. In a commentary on the Odes of Solomon, the oldest Christian hymns, I wrote:

"About 1960 a book of prayers that people really say in their hearts was shown to me by a friend. She particularly liked the very short one that simply said: 'Oh, God, won't You please stop this awful experiment of trying to make men like Christ?' These words embody the age-old struggle between God and man: the struggle of God to make man into god and the struggle of man to make God into man—or at least to make him give up and accept man as man and nothing more. In most instances the concept of divine incarnation or avatara is little more than man's pretence that God has become human and thereby somehow ratified and validated humanity and all its conditions and weaknesses. This is why the religions that worship supposed divine incarnations are such a mess, sinkholes of perverted intellect and emotion masquerading as 'devotion' and 'dedication' and 'service' to the liberated Sons of God whose example and wisdom are completely shoved into the background as the worship, adoration, and theologizing go on in a frenzy."

> **This comes to pass on this wise. Where the Truth always reigns, so that true perfect God and true perfect man are at one, and man so gives place to God, that God himself is there and yet the man too, and this same unity works continually, and does and leaves undone without any I, and Me, and Mine, and the like; behold, there is Christ, and nowhere else.**

"In him dwelleth all the fulness of the Godhead bodily" (Colossians 2:9), will in time be said about all of us, not just Jesus. And the Frankfurter agrees. About every one of us it is to be said: "The Word was made flesh, and dwelt among us, and we beheld his glory, the glory as of the only begotten of the Father, full of grace and truth" (John 1:14). Such is the power of God; a power in which we can participate if we will.

The Word of God is the Will of God. God speaks and it is. God speaks (wills) us and thereby the Word is made flesh in us and we become Words of God. David tells us: "I will declare the decree: the Lord hath said unto me, Thou art my Son; this day have I begotten thee" (Psalms 2:7). Saint Paul said: "I live; yet not I, but Christ liveth in me:" (Galatians 2:20).

In the New Testament Jesus is referred to as "the firstborn among many brethren" (Romans 8:29), "the firstborn of every creature" (Colossians 1:15), and simply "the firstborn" (Hebrews 12:23). If there is a firstborn, then there are to be other "borns" as well. That is why the esoteric Creed says: "We believe in Jesus Christ, the Lord of love and wisdom, first among His brethren, Who leads us to the glory of the Father, showing us the Way, the Truth, and the Life."

Now, seeing that here there is true perfect manhood, so there is a perfect perceiving and feeling of pleasure and pain, liking and disliking, sweetness and bitterness, joy and sorrow, and all that can be perceived and felt within and without.

A Christ is one in whom God dwells without diminishment or reservation. Therefore in every Christ God lives and experiences as a human being: a perfect human, but nevertheless human. In this union God is a perfected human being and that human being is a perfect god. Not only is Jesus true God and true Man, so is every son of God, one of the "just men made perfect" (Hebrews 12:23).

Now this is the true Christian Gospel. In the previous essay I have talked about those who encountered evil because of their negative beliefs. What other fate can those who deny the glorious truths of "Christ in you the hope of glory" expect to have but to be the subject of demonic persecution? On the other hand, think what will be the destiny of those who believe, accept and strive to be perfect sons of God?

"He that loveth Wisdom loveth life: and they that seek Her early shall be filled with joy. Teach me, O Lord, the way of Thy statutes: and I shall keep it unto the end. Give me understanding, and I shall keep Thy law: yea, I shall keep it with my whole heart. The path of the just is as the shining light: shining more and more unto the perfect day" (Common Gradual of the Liberal Catholic Liturgy).

And seeing that God is here made man, he is also able to perceive and feel love and hatred, evil and good and the like.

> As a man who is not God, feels and takes note of all that gives him pleasure and pain, and it pierces him to the heart, especially what offends him; so is it also when God and man are one, and yet God is the man; there everything is perceived and felt that is contrary to God and man. And since there man becomes nought, and God alone is everything, so is it with that which is contrary to man, and a sorrow to him. And this must hold true of God so long as a bodily and substantial life endures.

God is always at the core of sentient beings. "The Lord dwells in the hearts of all beings, causing them by his maya to revolve as if mounted on a machine. Fly unto him alone for refuge with your whole being. By that grace you shall attain supreme peace and the eternal abode" (Bhagavad Gita 18:61-62). So God is already in everyone, but he "becomes man" when a human attains total union with him. In that union man becomes God and God becomes man. This is possible only because in essence they are one from eternity. That is why we use the terms Self-realization and God-realization.

God experiences all the liberated person experiences, and the liberated one experiences God's consciousness. So whatever is done to such a one is done to God. This is a very serious matter. It is possible to create cosmic karma, positive or negative, according to our behavior toward him. It is true that those who killed Jesus killed God, but only in the way I have just described. Those who tried to kill Buddha were very lucky: they failed. Nevertheless, hating a liberated one is hating God, and insulting and wronging him is insulting and wronging God. Therefore terrible karmic consequences can accrue to those who encounter the sons of God, or immeasurably good karma.

"Man becomes nought" in that union because the spirit has never been a human, but has only taken on the body-costume of humanity. Then when that individual spirit attains union with God, all humanity is dissolved and only the divine nature remains. It is in this sense that a realized person has become nothing—actually "no thing". Certainly God has in him become all and he is henceforth god within God. The distinction, like the union, is eternal. But there is no difference or separation. This may seem like juggling words, but it is not. We need to understand as much as we can as we progress toward that goal.

> Furthermore, mark you, that the one Being in whom God and man are united, stands free of himself and of all things, and whatever is in him is there for God's sake and not for man's, or the creature's.

That is obvious, because the perfect one is no longer man but god within God. In such a one God is "All in All" (I Corinthians 15:28).

> For it is the property of God to be without this and that, and without Self and Me, and without equal or fellow; but it is the nature and property of the creature to seek itself and its own things, and this and that, here and there; and in all that it does and leaves undone its desire is to its own advantage and profit.

This is the diagnosis of the unenlightened person.

> Now where a creature or a man forsakes and comes out of himself and his own things, there God enters in with his own, that is, with himself.

And this is the prescribed remedy for all. As Rumi wrote:

A stone I died and rose again a plant.
A plant I died and rose an animal;
I died an animal and was born a man.
Why should I fear? What have I lost by death?
As man, death sweeps me from this world of men
That I may wear an angel's wings in heaven;
Yet e'en as angel may I not abide,
For nought abideth save the face of God.

Thus o'er the angels' world I wing my way
Onwards and upwards, unto boundless lights;
Then let me be as nought, for in my heart
Rings as a harp-song that we must return to Him.

And Oliver Wendell Holmes in *The Chambered Nautilus*:

Build thee more stately mansions, O my soul!
As the swift seasons roll!
Leave your low-vaulted past!
Let each new temple, nobler than the last,
Shut thee from heaven with a dome more vast,
Till you at length art free,
Leaving thine outgrown shell by life's unresting sea!

We leave all finite life behind and enter into Infinite Life forever.

DECEIVED DECEIVERS

(CHAPTER TWENTY FIVE)

Now, after that a man has walked in all the ways that lead him unto the truth, and exercised himself therein, not sparing his labour; now, as often and as long as he dreams that his work is altogether finished, and he is by this time quite dead to the world, and come out from Self and given up to God alone, behold! the Devil comes and sows his seed in the man's heart. From this seed spring two fruits; the one is spiritual fulness or pride, the other is false, lawless freedom. These are two sisters who love to be together.

The subject of spiritual deception, external and internal, is a grave one, indeed. The spiritually ignorant and the spiritually deluded (oftentimes the same) have always outnumbered the spiritually illumined and that is just the way the world is.

I have encountered a goodly number of deluded people through the years, some only slightly off center and some completely insane and dangerous. Every person I have met that has claimed "a kundalini experience" has been seriously unbalanced. And the sad thing is there seems to be no way to reach and help them. I once consulted a Christian esotericist (a priest) about helping a man who was literally disintegrating inside as a result of occult practice. He shook his head and told me: "People in that state can only be helped when they wholeheartedly beg for help, for they initiated the destructive process themselves and must desire to reverse it with their whole will." There was no alternative but to accept his diagnosis. I have never seen spiritual delusion dispelled completely.

The Teutonic priest lists four kinds of people that are guaranteed to become seriously deluded.

1) Those that believe they have attained complete enlightenment and need nothing more.

2) Those that believe they have conquered (mastered) all forces inner and outer and cannot be touched by the world.

3) Those that believe they no longer have an ego, but have transcended it.

4) Those that believe they either are the almighty God or are perfect images of the divine, and that all they say or do is inspired directly by God.

Some of these like to claim that they have a degree of realization and knowledge that has not heretofore been attained or possessed by any human being in history. Others claim to be reincarnations of Krishna or Buddha or Jesus, and some claim to have been all of them. I have met three Jesus Christs and one Virgin Mary (who was having an affair with one of the Jesuses). I have also known "a piece of the Divine Mother" (her description) that got broken off by accident in the early stages of creation. She was married to an incarnation of Saint Michael the Archangel. I also met Lucifer who claimed to be on the way back and up, and in the meantime wrote science fiction. (I am not joking or exaggerating about any of these.)

The Satanic Power overshadows and makes these people even crazier and more arrogant, and later on often drives them into the depths of depression and sometimes causes them to commit suicide.

Two things manifest in them, we are told: total pride and total disregard for any kind of restraint. Whatever pops into their head is the will of God (themselves) and they set about doing it. Their capacity for rationalizing their evident madness and foolishness is actually quite impressive. They become very good at being hopelessly deluded. Having actually attained a kind of ultimate condition, suicide seems quite reasonable to many of them, since there is nothing more they need or can do. (This is not uncommon in India among deluded yogis.) The "crazy wisdom" people are right in the midst of this.

Now, it begins on this wise: the Devil puffs up the man, till he thinks himself to have climbed the topmost pinnacle, and to have come so near to heaven, that he no longer needs Scripture, nor teaching, nor this nor that, but is altogether raised above any need.

Whereupon there arises a false peace and satisfaction with himself, and then it follows that he says or thinks: "Yes, now I am above all other men, and know and understand more than any one in the world; therefore it is certainly just and reasonable that I should be the lord and commander of all creatures, and that all creatures, and especially all men, should serve me and be subject unto me."

It is difficult to believe that anyone could fall into such madness, but it does not come from the deluded person. Oh, yes, the seeds came from within him, but Satan did the rest. Oftentimes evil human beings attach themselves to such a one and become his agents and assistants. I expect you will not be surprised if I tell you that some of these dupes of Satan are relatively unintelligent. So they need boosters. Hitler was a prime example. As the Catholic philosopher Dietrich von Hildebrand (who published a newspaper warning the Austrians about Hitler) pointed out, Hitler was a quintessential mediocrity. How did he succeed? Because he had a staff of people who were not mediocre and would dedicate themselves to his ideas and most of all to him. I have seen several unintelligent people who ruled over a tiny empire won and given to them by very intelligent and capable supporters whose motive was to work evil and incidentally win some power and money for themselves. But the evil is the prime motive.

We would be surprised if we could find out the number of people that right now are planning to be rulers of either the whole world or a large segment of it. Some of them have even been crowned in secret by their collaborators, and some of them have themselves "anointed" kings and emperors that they plan to run as puppets when their worldwide reign begins. Some of these groups even print their own money. There are certain religious organizations that teach as a dogma that they are "the religion of the future" and that their founder or key figure will one day be the only one worshipped throughout the world. Fortunately this is just a childish fantasy, yet there are false messiahs in training among them that will begin their own movement in time. The eventual fates of all these people are extremely bizarre. Yet many of them will have had a very destructive effect that will last even after their death.

> And then he seeks and desires the same, and takes it gladly from all creatures, especially men, and thinks himself well worthy of all this, and that it is his due, and looks on men as if they were the beasts of the field, and thinks himself worthy of all that ministers to his body and life and nature, in profit, or joy, or pleasure, or even pastime and amusement, and he seeks and takes it wherever he finds opportunity.

This is going on in many groups throughout the world.

> And whatever is done or can be done for him, seems him all too little and too poor, for he thinks himself worthy of still more and greater honor than can be rendered to him.

These leaders often hate their groupies because one day it dawns on them that without their staff and their followers they would be nothing at all, that they are completely dependent on their adorers without which they would be and would have nothing. Realizing their own smallness at last, they become enraged at their followers and become extremely abusive in many ways toward them. But since the fact of their total dependence is not changed (even though some of them have millions in Swiss bank accounts), they get no satisfaction and become increasingly bitter. Some vanish, some "retire," some are killed (poisoned usually) by their staff when they start getting out of control or they commit suicide which is covered up and turned into a major event for the future of the world. When Shelley wrote the poem *Ozymandias* he had political tyrants only in mind, but in our day many kinds of tyrants are reigning or trying to.

> And of all the men who serve him and are subject to him, even if they be downright thieves and murderers, he says nevertheless, that they have faithful, noble hearts, and have great love and faithfulness to the truth and to poor men. And such men are praised by him, and he seeks them and follows after them wherever they be.

This is standard. They form a gang and begin to exploit others. Look at the way those close to Hitler were minor deities in their own right. The leader is very good at inflating their egos, too. They create him and he creates them in a cycle of mutual advantage. One favorite activity of the spiritual dictators is the handing out of glory in the form of revelations as to who the leading thugs were in previous lives. After all it is only reasonable that the Greatest Teacher The World Has Ever Known should be surrounded by great figures from history, political and spiritual. One of the big guns of the Guru Boom in the 'sixties and 'seventies claimed that his brother was Jesus and his mother the Virgin Mary. They both sued him eventually for their share of the loot.

Since the world began this lunacy has been going on in many forms.

> But he who does not order himself according to the will of these high-minded men, nor is subject unto them, is not sought after by them, nay, more likely blamed and spoken ill of, even though he were as holy as St. Peter himself.

To not bow before the Latest and Best deity of humanity does not go unnoticed, and usually not unpunished in some way. However, the moment it is realized that someone sees through "the painted veil" then that person is thenceforth invisible in their sacred realm. Often it is not allowed to even speak their name. Since the Inmost One is of course positive at all times, any attack would be inappropriate and might raise questions. So silence is the reaction as the Frankfurter points out.

A friend of mine got on the black list of a cult organization after having been a major official for some years. If his name was brought up or inquiry made, the mouthpieces would says things like: "Well, you notice he left our organization." (He was expelled in secret; he did not leave.) "He knows what he did." (So no false accusations had to be made.) "He overstepped himself." (?????)

> **And seeing that this proud and puffed-up spirit thinks that he needs neither Scripture, nor instruction, nor anything of the kind, therefore she gives no heed to the admonitions, order, laws and precepts of the holy Christian Church, nor to the Sacraments, but mocks at them and at all men who walk according to these ordinances and hold them in reverence.**

Many leaders in the spiritual carnival sideshow have taught the need to break out of old forms and forge new ways for the New Age (which they are bringing in) and boasted of having discarded all traditions and texts; that nothing more needs to be said. A favorite rationale is that traditional ways make it hard to break away and receive the new revelation. Just buy the leader's books and videos. (The books are often ghost-written.)

> **Hereby we may plainly see that those two sisters dwell together.**

Yes; they are inseparable. Sometimes one paves the way for the other, but once united they are always together.

> **Moreover since this sheer pride thinks to know and understand more than all men besides, therefore she chooses to prate more than all other men, and would fain have her opinions and speeches to be alone regarded and listened to, and counts all that others think and say to be wrong, and holds it in derision as a folly.**

I could make a list right now of contemporary leaders, especially in religion, and most especially in the realm of Indian philosophy and yoga, who embody this description in every detail. Although they are rivals they often have a backroom agreement to keep silent about each other. They occasionally get together and palaver about those that do not belong to their cabal but whose antics if fully revealed would have a detrimental effect on all of them in a kind of guilt by genre if not association. The best known (at the moment) acts as a kind of Godfather who dispenses favors to those who keep a low profile in his territory, the least visible the better. In exchange, as I say, various favors are given, many as least visible as possible, though photos and book endorsements are passed around quite freely among them.

Moreover since this sheer pride thinks to know and understand more than all men besides, therefore she chooses to prate more than all other men. The volume of "teaching" produced by these people is often prodigious. Since each of them alone really knows the whole truth, they have to get the word out so the world can know it, too. Many times the releasing of a book or an audio or video brings in a new era–or so they say. Of course all their talks are inspired, some of them making a point of not planning ahead what they will say, but just opening their mouth and letting "the teaching" out. One thing they all have in common: their teachings have no practical value but consist only of unapplicable "knowledge." As they say in Kentucky: The empty wagon rattles the most.

And would fain have her opinions and speeches to be alone regarded and listened to. Absolutely. One mark of a cult/cultist is the insistence that only the leader's words should be studied. Otherwise the cult members will "get confused." Sometimes dire consequences are predicted if "the purity of the teachings" is not kept and they lose "attunement" with the teacher by looking anywhere but in their association. Eventually, however positive their public face, they begin threatening their followers with harm from either evil people (anyone that does not agree with them or belong to their organization) or evil spirits if they do not stay safely in the master's fold. For a true picture of the paranoia harbored by all these teachers and imparted to their followers, see the book *Call No Man Master* by Joyce Collin-Smith.

And counts all that others think and say to be wrong, and holds it in derision as a folly. This is of course a trait of all spiritual slave-takers whatever the era or ilk, including some Indian gurus and ashrams. As I mentioned before, one mark of a false teacher is the insistence that they alone—usually for the first time in history—see the whole picture and can tell others about it. Apparently the world has been waiting all this time to have things cleared up by them. Beforehand it was impossible. Smart Shoppers take note!

POOR IN SPIRIT AND HUMBLE

(CHAPTER TWENTY SIX)

Having shown us the situation and peril of the proud and self-serving who set themselves up as leaders and instructors of humanity, the Teutonic priest-knight turns to the opposite spiritual personality type which he urges us to emulate.

> **But it is quite otherwise where there is poorness of spirit, and true humility; and it is so because it is found and known of a truth that a man, of himself and his own power, is nothing, has nothing, can do and is capable of nothing but only infirmity and evil.**

We will be in trouble if we take this in the modern sense of "sinful man." What the author is saying is that where there is humility and awareness that all we have has come from God, that there is nothing separate or outside of God, and that our ego, being blind and bound, can only lead us astray and bring us into grave trouble and danger, then true virtue will prevail. Then salvation and not destruction will be possible for us. The heaven and the hell we are to seek or shun is not outside us, but inside. Heaven is spirit consciousness and hell is ego consciousness. The external realms of heaven and hell await the individual solely on the basis of his inner consciousness, not mere thought or action, but the level of consciousness, the level of evolution.

> **Hence follows that the man finds himself altogether unworthy of all that has been or ever will be done for him, by God or the creatures, and that he is a debtor to God and also to all the**

creatures in God's stead, both to bear with, and to labour for, and to serve them.

We must understand that everything is from God, either directly or through his agents, that it is a matter of cause and effect: of karma. Yet it is not mechanical and impersonal, it is a manifestation of love on God's part because it is working toward our betterment. The secret is this: Everything is ours when we truly see that "now are we the sons of God, and it doth not yet appear what we shall be: but we know that, when he shall appear, we shall be like him; for we shall see him as he is" (I John 3:2). Nothing is ours when we think that we deserve everything and are being wronged if we do not get it. For in the one instance it is the spirit that is alive to the realities of life, and in the other it is the ego that understands nothing but its negative thoughts and will. The ego screams about its rights, but the spirit acknowledges its responsibilities.

And therefore he does not in any wise stand up for his own rights, but from the humility of his heart he says, "It is just and reasonable that God and all creatures should be against me, and have a right over me, and to me, and that I should not be against any one, nor have a right to anything."

Again, the Frankfurter is not advocating self-loathing or self-depre-cation, but the realization that all things are the gift of God and never a fulfillment of our "rights." Of course, without the knowledge and under-standing of karma and reincarnation nothing in our life makes any sense. Ignorance is a breeding ground for misunderstanding, rebellion and lim-itless negativity. Even if made into some kind of philosophical, religious or social system, it still is false and destructive. It opens the gates of hell and closes the gates of heaven. And it is all our own choice. There is no one to blame but us.

I must tell you that this is not some extreme idea, an exaggeration. The various "peace churches," those that truly and sincerely oppose war and participation in war, often act in accordance with this principle. For example, I know of one pacifist church whose members will not engage in lawsuits. More than once in their history unscrupulous people have taken over their meeting-places and claimed ownership. They simply went elsewhere and found or built another meeting-place. When sued they will not engage an attorney but will come to the court and accept whatever happens. Some of these people I have known personally.

> Hence it follows that the man does not and will not crave or beg for anything, either from God or the creatures, beyond mere needful things, and for those only with shamefacedness, as a favor and not as a right.
>
> And he will not minister unto or gratify his body or any of his natural desires, beyond what is needful, nor allow that any should help or serve him except in case of necessity, and then always in trembling; for he has no right to anything and therefore he thinks himself unworthy of anything.
>
> So likewise all his own discourse, ways, words and works seem to this man a thing of nought and a folly. Therefore he speaks little, and does not take upon himself to admonish or rebuke any, unless he be constrained thereto by love or faithfulness towards God, and even then he does it in fear, and so little as may be.

This is all very clear in light of what has gone before.

> Moreover, when a man has this poor and humble spirit, he comes to see and understand aright, how that all men are bent upon themselves, and inclined to evil and sin, and that on this account it is needful and profitable that there be order, customs, law and precepts, to the end that the blindness and foolishness of men may be corrected, and that vice and wickedness may be kept under, and constrained to seemliness. For without ordinances, men would be much more mischievous and ungovernable than dogs and cattle. And few have come to the knowledge

of the truth but what have begun with holy practices and ordinances, and exercised themselves therein so long as they knew
nothing more nor better.

*Moreover, when a man has this poor and humble spirit, he comes to see and
understand aright, how that all men are bent [turned in] upon themselves, and
inclined to evil and sin.* The awakening person must first awaken to that
enlightenment which lies beyond him at the moment. But before he can
reach out for it he must understand the root of all wrong and the root of
all right. Self-centered egotism is the root of all wrong, and humble awe
before God is the root of all right.

Every evil is ego-involvement in some form. When the yogi finds his
mind seemingly running everywhere, if he will look closely he will see
that it is simply running after the ego, after the false self and everything it
is bound up with. Simple inattention and wandering of the mind is not
at all simple: it comes from a pernicious self-interest that cannot endure
fixing the mind on God to the exclusion of all else. That is why meditation
and the inner search is the final step: the ignorant person tries everything
else in desperation first. The egocentric mind is very clever and extremely
creative in running away from any confrontation with God.

Lukewarm yoga practice is not enough. The yogi must ruthlessly cut
off interest in anything that deflects from the path to God. He must
refuse to be distracted by the blathering of the idiot mind. "Abandoning
those desires whose origins lie in one's intention—all of them without
exception—also completely restraining the many senses by the mind, with
the buddhi firmly controlled, with the mind fixed on the Self, he should
gain quietude by degrees. Let him not think of any extraneous thing
whatever. Whenever the unsteady mind, moving here and there, wanders
off, he should subdue and hold it back and direct it to the Self's control"
(Bhagavad Gita 6:24-26).

*And that on this account it is needful and profitable that there be order,
customs, law and precepts, to the end that the blindness and foolishness of
men may be corrected, and that vice and wickedness may be kept under, and
constrained to seemliness.* Discipline is a necessity, and the yogi must realize

that the "order, customs, law and precepts" which the ignorant like to refer to as "all that" in a dismissive way, is absolutely mandatory.

The masters have gone before us on the way to liberation, and they did so by following the precepts of those that went before them. Before setting a foot on the path they learned what would be expected, even demanded, of them if they were to persevere to the end and be free. There are laws that govern spiritual life just as there are laws that govern other pursuits and endeavors.

The sages of India have left for us a tremendous amount of instruction on how to go about preparing ourselves for the journey, and all the rules of the road that we will have to know and adopt if we really want to get somewhere. Law and Order are companions on our way to enlightenment. I knew a very foolish man who had been a very foolish child. He boasted to me that as a child whenever he got something which required assembly the very first thing he did was to throw the instructions away. He thought that was very cute and clever.

There is no such thing as a viable spiritual endeavor that is not conducted according to Tradition, and I do mean that capital T. Those who do not acquaint themselves with the traditions behind yoga will never get anywhere. When Patanjali listed the steps in yoga, the very first were Yama and Niyama. Until they are being worked on diligently there is no need to go on to any further steps. This is why so many yogis wander off into the desert of ignorance and confusion and wind up spiritual casualties.

For without ordinances, men would be much more mischievous and ungovernable than dogs and cattle. Certainly the complex minds of human beings can come up with wrong and foolish acts that animals would not even stumble upon by accident. Therefore "order, customs, law and precepts" are necessary to curb human ingenuity in thinking up more and more destructive things.

And few have come to the knowledge of the truth but what have begun with holy practices and ordinances, and exercised themselves therein so long as they knew nothing more nor better. Spiritual life is not a hit-or-miss matter, but develops according to exact laws. Unhappily most "spiritual" organizations have no clue at all regarding genuine spiritual life, so they just mess up people's minds and lives, and disaster results eventually.

The Frankfurter values the various disciplines, but he refers to "more" and "better" things that are needed to pursue a viable spiritual life. These are the things that only those who have succeeded in their search are able to pass on to others. Such persons are few indeed and hard to recognize.

> **Therefore one who is poor in spirit and of a humble mind does not despise or make light of law, order, precepts and holy customs, nor yet of those who observe and cleave wholly to them, but with loving pity and gentle sorrow, cries: "Almighty Father, Thou Eternal Truth, I make my lament unto Thee, and it grieves Thy Spirit too, that through man's blindness, infirmity, and sin, that is made needful and must be, which in deed and truth were neither needful nor right." For those who are perfect are under no law.**

Many spiritual practices would not be needed if people were not "fallen" or spiritually crippled. We have to begin where we are at the moment, so we must not egotistically think that we are above or beyond the traditional ways of religion. That attitude is a common trait of the spiritually unqualified. We take medicine so we can get well and stop taking it. It is the same with spiritual practices. Certainly we want to eventually have no need for them, but until we are completely well in spirit they are very necessary for us.

Why does the author tell us that we need to feel regret at needing spiritual disciplines? Because many people love to stack up all kinds of practices and observances, thinking that the more they do the more spiritual they are. And they become very pharisaical toward those who are not as involved as they are with such things. The more medicine you take, the more it indicates that you are sick. Therefore the more we engage in various disciplines the more we are indicating our advanced level of inner sickness. We are not virtuous, we are showing spiritual good sense. Unfortunately I have seen people use their observances to make themselves seem dedicated and spiritual and to imply that those not so observant are in the wrong. Ego is very creative in its ways, so we must be ever watchful.

> So order, laws, precepts and the like are merely an admonition to men who understand nothing better and know and perceive not wherefore all law and order is ordained.

Without understanding, nothing we do can benefit us. It will just be useless activity that has no meaning. Knowing what we are doing is a prime necessity in spiritual life.

> And the perfect accept the law along with such ignorant men as understand and know nothing better, and practice it with them, to the intent that they may be restrained thereby, and kept from evil ways, or if it be possible, brought to something higher.

In the Bhagavad Gita Krishna tells us: "For the maintenance of the world, as an example you should act.... The wise should act, intending to maintain the welfare of the world" (Bhagavad Gita 3:20, 25)

> Behold! all that we have said of poverty and humility is so of a truth, and we have the proof and witness thereof in the pure life of Christ, and in his words. For he both practiced and fulfilled every work of true humility and all other virtues, as shines forth in his holy life, and he says also expressly: "Learn from Me, for I am gentle and lowly in heart, and you will find rest for your souls" (Matthew 11:29).

Jesus is our pattern because he was at first just as we are: a limited human being. Yet he rose to the heights of divine consciousness, and in him God manifested "all the fulness of the Godhead bodily" (Colossians 2:9. See *Robe of Light*). If Jesus did it, everyone can do it. This is the true message of the Gospel of Christ. We must face up to this challenge and "know that, when he shall appear [be revealed], we shall be like him" (I John 3:2).

> **Moreover he did not despise and set at nought the law and the commandments, nor yet the men who are under the law. He says: "Think not that I am come to destroy the law, or the prophets: I am not come to destroy, but to fulfil" (Matthew 5:17). But he says further, that to keep them is not enough, we must press forward to what is higher and better, as is indeed true.**

Spiritual hypocrites like to go on about "mere externals" that they claim have no value. But those externals are the very things that open up the way to the inner kingdom. As I said, we must start the journey from the very place we are at this moment. Those who think they are beyond externals have not yet come to the point where they can comprehend them.

It is a sad truth that Westerners are continually demanding to know what is the least they can do. Even in sacred ritual they are seeking for the minimum needed to make it effective. Pretending to be interested in the essence of things they are assiduously avoiding their spiritual obligations. They always want to know the least they can do and yet be acceptable. Such an attitude of arrogant contempt is a guarantee of their spiritual ruin.

Consider the terrible condition Saint Mary Magdalene was in when she met Jesus. She was not only living a life of dissolution, she was possessed by evil spirits (Mark 16:9). Yet, as Jesus said: "Her sins, which are many, are forgiven; for she loved much: but to whom little is forgiven, the same loveth little" (Luke 7:47). And that love was shown toward the end of his earthly life when she "came having an alabaster box of ointment of spikenard very precious; and she brake the box, and poured it on his head" (Mark 14:3). The Himalayan Balsam was incredibly expensive because every country it was brought through levied a high tax on it. Consequently it was kept in a kind of alabaster bottle with a tiny opening so it could be dispensed a drop at a time. But Saint Mary's love could not tolerate a drop by drop offering, but broke off the top and poured the whole thing out upon Jesus' head. It must be the same with us.

> He says: "Unless your righteousness exceeds the righteousness of the scribes and Pharisees, you will by no means enter the kingdom of heaven" (Matthew 5:20). For the law forbids evil works, but Christ condemns also evil thoughts; the law allows us to take vengeance on our enemies, but Christ commands us to love them. The law forbids not the good things of this world, but he counsels us to despise them.

External observance of virtue is needed, but to that we must add the internal observance, for together they purify and correct the mind and heart. If our inner life is not conformed to Christ, then we are nothing at all. We must do the maximum, not the minimum. Our life must be a total offering, not a grudging eking out of the least we can do.

> And he has set his seal upon all he said, with his own holy life; for he taught nothing that he did not fulfill in work, and he kept the law and was subject unto it to the end of his mortal life. Likewise St. Paul says: "Christ was made under the law, to redeem them that were under the law" (Galatians 4:4). That is, that he might bring them to something higher and nearer to himself. He said again, "The Son of man came not to be ministered unto, but to minister" (Matthew 20:28).
>
> In a word: in Christ's life and words and works, we find nothing but true, pure humility and poverty such as we have set forth. And therefore where God dwells in a man, and the man is a true follower of Christ, it will be, and must be, and ought to be the same.

This cannot be honestly denied. But it is also true that, as Saint Teresa of Avila said to Jesus, his friends are few. "Because strait is the gate, and narrow is the way, which leadeth unto life, and few there be that find it" (Matthew 7:14).

> But where there is pride, and a haughty spirit, and a light, careless mind, Christ is not, nor any true follower of his.

This is an awesome truth and we should examine ourselves in its light.

Christ says also: "Blessed are the poor in spirit" (that is, those who are truly humble), "for theirs is the kingdom of Heaven." And thus we find it of a truth, where God is made man. For in Christ and in all his true followers, there must needs be thorough humility and poorness of spirit, a lowly retiring disposition, and a heart laden with a secret sorrow and mourning, so long as this mortal life lasts. And he who dreams otherwise is deceived, and deceives others with him as aforesaid. Therefore nature and Self always avoid this life, and cling to a life of false freedom and ease, as we have said.

Where God is being made man in someone's life, there is always a yearning, a nostalgia, for perfect life in God, a life far beyond and above this world. Therefore Jesus said: "The foxes have holes, and the birds of the air have nests; but the Son of man hath not where to lay his head" upon this earth (Matthew 8:20). The true disciple of Christ never finds rest and fulfillment in the things and ways of this world, but ever looks beyond it to a Reality undreamed of by most of humanity.

Behold! now comes an Adam or an Evil Spirit, wishing to justify himself and make excuse, and says: "You will almost have it that Christ was bereft of self and the like, yet he spoke often of himself, and glorified himself in this and that." Answer: when a man in whom the truth works, has and ought to have a will towards anything, his will and endeavor and works are for no end, but that the truth may be seen and manifested; and this will was in Christ, and to this end, words and works were needful. And what Christ did because it was the most profitable and best means thereunto, he no more took unto himself than anything else that happened.

Jesus had no "life of his own" but lived in and for God. He did not just accept the cross, he pursued it, because he knew it was the door to life, to resurrection into Infinite Being and Consciousness. This was the great secret he shared with his disciples. And he wills to do the same with us. For he asks of each one: "Are ye able to drink of the cup that I shall drink of, and to be baptized with the baptism that I am baptized with?" (Matthew 20:22).

> **Do you say now: "Then there was a Wherefore in Christ"? I answer, if you were to ask the sun, "Why do you shine?" he would say: "I must shine, and cannot do otherwise, for it is my nature and property; but this my property, and the light I give, is not of myself, and I do not call it mine." So likewise is it with God and Christ and all who are godly and belong unto God. In them is no willing, nor working nor desiring but has for its end, goodness as goodness, for the sake of goodness, and they have no other Wherefore than this.**

It is our eternal, divine nature that must ultimately be manifested in us, just as it was in Christ. "When all things shall be subdued unto him, then shall the Son also himself be subject unto him that put all things under him, that God may be all in all" (I Corinthians 15:28).

When All is Nothing and Nothing is All

(Chapter Twenty Seven)

Now, according to what has been said, you must observe that when we say, as Christ also says, that we ought to resign and forsake all things, this is not to be taken in the sense that a man is neither to do nor to purpose anything; for a man must always have something to do and to order so long as he lives.

This is very important, because some things previously said could cause a person to mistake the author's meaning and assume that we are to be indifferent to all things and so detached from them that we would barely be alive, and certainly not acting as though we have obligations and duties, which all human beings do.

But we are to understand by it that the union with God stands not in any man's powers, in his working or abstaining, perceiving or knowing, nor in that of all the creatures taken together.

We should realize that mere action in and of itself counts for nothing in the matter of living in true harmony and union with God.

Now what is this union? It is that we should be of a truth purely, simply, and wholly at one with the One Eternal Will of God, or altogether without will, so that the created will should flow out into the Eternal Will, and be swallowed up and lost therein, so that the Eternal Will alone should do and leave undone in us.

This is an incredibly high ideal. It can be realized, but not in a moment or effortlessly. Since God and man are spirit beings, pure consciousness, the priest is pointing us to the need for our consciousness to be in harmony and then in perfect union with the divine will, that our will should reflect God's will; that through purification and discipline our will should become a perfect reflection of the cosmic will and mirror its purpose: transmutation of the human into the Divine.

Now mark what may help or further us towards this end. Behold, neither exercises, nor words, nor works, nor any creature nor creature's work can do this. In this wise therefore must we renounce and forsake all things, that we must not imagine or suppose that any words, works, or exercises, any skill or cunning or any created thing can help or serve us thereto.

We must understand that no external action can accomplish this necessary perfection. Nothing that is "of us" means anything in this, either. All our endeavor must be on the highest level to succeed. Realizing our divine nature, finite though it be, we must continually live in that perspective, constantly aware of God's assurance to us: "You are gods" (Psalms 82:6; John 10:34). We must continually invoke that spirit consciousness. We must be yogis.

Therefore we must allow these things to be what they are, and enter into the union with God. Yet outward things must be, and we must do and refrain so far as is necessary, especially we must sleep and wake, walk and stand still, speak and be silent and much more of the like. These must go on so long as we live.

Although we are not aware of it in our ignorance, we are actively working to keep our distance from God and to maintain our separation and our "humanity" in order to avoid the divine life that is our destiny. So the master is teaching us to let our lesser self alone and cling to our higher self at all times. There is no way our lesser self can produce any significant progress in the yoga life. Instead it must all come from the highest level of our existence: our eternal spirit.

God is beyond all conceptions or intellectual grasp. Therefore we must leave them aside, even though exoteric religion is made of such things exclusively, and elevate our awareness through constant invocation of the Divine Consciousness. We must follow the mystical life of the spirit, continually reminding ourselves that "now are we the sons of God" (I John 3:2), whose sole duty is to manifest that ever-present state in its fullness so that we, too may hear the witness of the Father to us as well as to Jesus: "This is my beloved son, in whom I am well pleased" (Matthew 3:17).

Moving and Immoveable

(Chapter Twenty Eight)

Now, when this union truly comes to pass and becomes established, the inward man stands henceforward immoveable in this union; and God suffers the outward man to be moved hither and thither, from this to that, of such things as are necessary and right. So that the outward man says in sincerity "I have no will to be or not to be, to live or die, to know or not to know, to do or to leave undone and the like; but I am ready for all that is to be, or ought to be, and obedient thereunto, whether I have to do or to endure." And thus the outward man has no Wherefore or purpose, but only to do his part to further the Eternal Will.

Here we see that the human being has two distinct parts: the outer and the inner. And when the right state has been attained, the outer is movable, often to a great degree, but the inner is immovable. Therefore the two do not reflect one another. This is because the outer man is in the relative world and experiences life as immanent in the world. The inner man, on the other hand, dwells in the transcendental realm and cannot be touched or influenced by the relative. The sages of India have known this through the ages, and furthermore they know what to do about it and how to get the two established in their right state: yoga. Those who are perfected in yoga can say with the fullest meaning: "For to me, to live is Christ" (Philippians 1:21)–that is, Ishwara, for Christ and Ishwara are the same.

For it is perceived of a truth, that the inward man shall stand immoveable, and that it is needful for the outward man to be moved.

This is the right state for the enlightened human being. The Bhagavad Gita makes it very clear.

"Not by abstaining from actions does a man attain the state beyond action, and not by mental renunciation alone does he approach to perfection. Truly, no one for even a moment exists without doing action. Each person is compelled to perform action, even against his will, by the gunas born of prakriti. He who by the mind controls the senses, and yet is unattached while engaging action's organs in action, is superior.

"Perform your duty, for action is far better than non-action. Even maintaining your body cannot be done without action. The world is bound by the actions not done for sake of sacrifice. Hence for sacrifice you should act without attachment. He who here on the earth turns not the wheel thus set in motion, lives full of sense delights, maliciously and uselessly.

"He who is content only in the Self, who is satisfied in the Self, who is pleased only in the Self: for him there is no need to act. He has no purpose at all in action or in non-action, and he has no need of anyone for any purpose whatsoever. Therefore, constantly unattached perform that which is your duty. Indeed by unattached action man attains the Supreme.

"As the unwise act, attached to action, so the wise should act, unattached, intending to maintain the welfare of the world. One should not unsettle the minds of the ignorant attached to action. The wise should cause them to enjoy all actions, himself engaged in their performance.

"In all situations actions are performed by the gunas of Prakriti. Those with ego-deluded mind think: 'I am the doer.' But he who knows the truth about the gunas and action thinks: 'The gunas act in the gunas.' Thinking thus, he is not attached. Those deluded by the gunas of prakriti are attached to the actions of the gunas. The knower of the whole truth should not disturb the foolish of partial knowledge. Renouncing all actions in me, intent on the Supreme Spirit, free from desire and 'mine,' free from the 'fever' of delusion and grief: fight!

"Those who constantly follow this teaching of mine, full of faith, not opposing it, they are released from the bondage of their actions. But those opposing and not practicing my teaching, confusing all knowledge, know them to be lost and mindless.

"One acts according to one's own prakriti–even the wise man does so. Beings follow their own prakriti; what will restraint accomplish?

"Attraction and aversion are inherent in the contact of the senses with sense-objects. One should not come under the power of these two–they are indeed his enemies.

"Better is one's swadharma, though deficient, than the swadharma of another well performed. Better is death in one's own swadharma. The swadharma of another brings danger" (Bhagavad Gita 3:4-5, 7-9, 16-19, 25-35).

> And if the inward man have any Wherefore in the actions of the outward man, he says only that such things must be and ought to be, as are ordained by the Eternal Will. And where God himself dwells in the man, it is thus; as we plainly see in Christ.

The man of wisdom lives his life simply and directly, caring nothing for what comes or goes externally, but anchored in the unmoving spirit to such a degree that the life or death of the body has no meaning and makes no difference in his consciousness.

> Moreover, where there is this union, which is the offspring of a Divine light and dwells in its beams, there is no spiritual pride or irreverent spirit, but boundless humility, and a lowly broken [contrite] heart; also an honest blameless walk, justice, peace, content, and all that is of virtue must needs be there.

Here we see the interior state of the perfect man.

> Where they are not, there is no right union, as we have said. For just as neither this thing nor that can bring about or further this union, so there is nothing which has power to frustrate or hinder it, save the man himself with his self-will, that does him this great wrong. Of this be well assured.

Where the listed virtues are not found, the divine order is not found, either. The sole obstacle to the fulfillment of this ideal is the individual himself, and the sole thing needed for success is the individual as well.

"Behold, I have set before thee an open door, and no man can shut it" (Revelation 3:8).

BEYOND ALL

(CHAPTER THIRTY)

Some say further, that we can and ought to get beyond all virtue, all custom and order, all law, precepts and seemliness, so that all these should be laid aside, thrown off and set at nought.

This is a favorite idea among those Westerners who have "turned East" and seek to use Oriental philosophy as justification for their contempt and aversion for discipline–especially that which would limit or eliminate their indulgence in material things. This is their false idea of freedom, even though it actually entails total bondage to earth and earthliness.

"That they may recover themselves out of the snare of the devil, who are taken captive by him at his will" (II Timothy 2:26), is what Saint Paul says is the only hope for the slaves of the world.

Further: "This know also, that in the last days perilous times shall come. For men shall be lovers of their own selves, covetous, boasters, proud, blasphemers, disobedient to parents, unthankful, unholy, without natural affection, trucebreakers, false accusers, incontinent, fierce, despisers of those that are good, traitors, heady, highminded, lovers of pleasures more than lovers of God; having a form of godliness, but denying the power thereof: *from such turn away*. Ever learning, and never able to come to the knowledge of the truth. Now as Jannes and Jambres withstood Moses, so do these also resist the truth: men of corrupt minds, reprobate concerning the faith. But they shall proceed no further: for their folly shall be manifest unto all men, as theirs also was" (II Timothy 3:1-9). So all we need do is wait and they shall themselves reveal their perversity and evil ways. This has been my experience from childhood. I have seen a lot of masks drop and a lot of demon faces revealed.

Herein there is some truth, and some falsehood.

The cleverest form of evil is that which mixes truth with falsehood. And so it is with these people that decry all discipline and denial of the ways of the world.

> **Behold and mark: Christ was greater than his own life, and above all virtue, custom, ordinances and the like. For Christ was and is above them on this wise, that his words, and works, and ways, his doings and refrainings, his speech and silence, his sufferings, and whatsoever happened to him, were not forced upon him, neither did He need them, neither were they of any profit to himself.**

The life of Jesus was not lived for himself, but for our benefit, as an opening of the way for us to attain theosis (deification). Before becoming incarnate two thousand years ago, Jesus had passed through all the levels of evolution and was perfected in them. Therefore he transcended them and entered into the depths of God as a Son of God. He became incarnate in God and God became incarnate in him so all difference was no more, although their eternal distinction remained.

Then, fulfilling the will of the Father, Jesus the Son once more took up earthly incarnation—not for himself but for us. That is why the author tells us that "Christ was greater than his own life."

> **It was and is the same with all manner of virtue, order, laws, decency, and the like; for all that may be reached by them is already in Christ to perfection.**

What we must realize is that the attainment of a master means nothing to us if we are not engaged in reaching the identical attainment ourselves. Jesus has not done it for us. He showed that it could be done, but we must be our own proof of the infinite potential that is inherent in each sentient being.

In this sense, that saying of St. Paul is true and receives its fulfillment, "As many as are led by the Spirit of God, they are the sons of God," "and are not under the law, but under grace" (Romans 8:14, and 6:14). That means, man need not teach them what they are to do or abstain from; for their Master, that is, the Spirit of God, shall verily teach them what is needful for them to know.

How is this possible? Because our very existence is rooted in God; we exist because he exists. The Spirit, the Breath, of God is in each one of us, moving us toward the goal of divine perfection. We are a part of God, otherwise we could never ascend to the heights of existence in God. This truth must always kept in mind: "I can do all things through Christ which strengtheneth me" (Philippians 4:13) because I am one with Christ, with Ishwara the Lord of Cosmic Evolution. From eternity my destiny has been inherent in me. The life in me is the Life in all things.

Likewise they do not need that men should give them precepts, or command them to do right and not to do wrong, and the like; for the same admirable Master who teaches them what is good or not good, what is higher and lower, and in short leads them into all truth, He reigns also within them, and bids them to hold fast that which is good, and to let the rest go, and to him they give ear.

Emily Brontë has made all this clear:

O God within my breast,
Almighty, ever-present Deity!
Life, that in me has rest,
As I, undying Life, have power in Thee!

Vain are the thousand creeds
That move men's hearts: unutterably vain;

Worthless as withered weeds,
Or idlest froth amid the boundless main,

To waken doubt in one
Holding so fast by Thy infinity,
So surely anchored on
The steadfast rock of Immortality.

With wide-embracing love
Thy Spirit animates eternal years,
Pervades and broods above,
Changes, sustains, dissolves, creates, and rears.

Though earth and moon were gone,
And suns and universes ceased to be,
And Thou wert left alone,
Every existence would exist in Thee.

There is not room for Death,
Nor atom that his might could render void:
Thou—you art Being and Breath,
And what you art may never be destroyed.

Behold! in this sense they need not to wait upon any law, either to teach or to command them. In another sense also they need no law; namely, in order to seek or win something thereby or get any advantage for themselves. For whatever help toward eternal life, or furtherance in the way everlasting, they might obtain from the aid, or counsel, or words, or works of any creature, they possess already beforehand. Behold! in this sense also it is true, that we may rise above all law and virtue, and also above the works and knowledge and powers of any creature.

For we are not "creature," but one with the Creator.

GOD AND CREATION

(CHAPTER THIRTY ONE)

But that other thing which they affirm, how that we ought to throw off and cast aside the life of Christ, and all laws and commandments, customs and order and the like, and pay no heed to them, but despise and make light of them, is altogether false and a lie.

It is intriguing how many times in the history of Christianity this idea has come up in some form or another. Both Luther and Rasputin taught that there is no forgiveness of sins without repentance, so to ensure our repentance is profound and sincere we should sin as much as we can: then we will repent and be justified. As my mother used to say: "All those who believe that, stand on your head." But a lot of people have pretended they did so their sin would appear to be righteousness.

It is absolutely true that we must go beyond good and evil. That is, we must no longer do something because it is good and doing so will get us a reward, nor should we avoid doing something because it is evil and will bring us suffering and even destruction. Those motives are centered on the ego. What we must do is ascend in consciousness and become so transformed inwardly that we always do good because it is our nature to do so, and never do evil because it is contrary to our nature to do so. We should live the Christ-life spontaneously, saying truthfully: "I live; yet not I, but Christ liveth in me" (Galatians 2:20). This is the right view.

Now some may say; "Since neither Christ nor others can ever gain anything, either by a Christian life, or by all these exercises and ordinances, and the like, nor turn them to any

account, seeing that they possess already all that can be had through them, what cause is there why they should not henceforth eschew them altogether? Must they still retain and practice them?"

The reasoning is quite obvious; and it is quite obviously nonsense. This is the trouble with things that seem logical or make sense. That is why the masters of all eras have told us that divine wisdom is far beyond words and concepts. This is why yoga does not weave webs of philosophical or theological teachings, but purifies and transforms the consciousness of the yogi. The yogi does not just believe or teach the truth, he *becomes* the truth.

Behold, you must look narrowly into this matter. There are two kinds of Light; the one is true and the other is false. The true light is that Eternal Light which is God; or else it is a created light, but yet divine, which is called grace. And these are both the true Light.

There is a vast difference between the Western and Eastern view of the nature of "grace." The West has formulated definitions of different forms of grace and juggled them around, mostly confusing everyone. The Eastern Christian view is quite simple: The grace of God *is* God; that is, the grace of God is direct contact with God and the changes it effects. Grace is not a thing; it is an experience. It is God-experience in varying degrees. That is not just blessedly simple, it is blessedly true.

So is the false light Nature or of Nature. But why is the first true, and the second false? This we can better perceive than say or write.

Nature—Maya—is giving a false appearance, so its light is false even though at its inmost level the Light of God is present as its essential substance. For in the final analysis everything is God.

> To God, as Godhead, appertain neither will, nor knowledge, nor manifestation, nor anything that we can name, or say, or conceive.

In essence God is transcendent and therefore No Thing. As a consequence nothing can be said about God and nothing can be attributed to God.

> But to God as God, it belongs to express himself, and know and love himself, and to reveal himself to himself; and all this without any creature. And all this rests in God as a substance but not as a working, so long as there is no creature. And out of this expressing and revealing of himself unto himself, arises the distinction of Persons.

But to God as God, it belongs to express himself, and know and love himself, and to reveal himself to himself; and all this without any creature. In the West all kinds of "why does God do?" questions are bandied around. Naturally, "Why does God create the world?" is a popular one and a great deal of very silly answers are thought up. In the East, whether Hindu, Taoist, Buddhist or Christian, the same answer is given: *Because it is his nature to do so.* And the Teutonic priest-knight holds the same view. It is innate in God to do all the things he lists. And he "reveals himself to himself" in all beings because he is at the core of their very existence. All this he does directly and immediately, without the agency of any creature.

And all this rests in God as a substance but not as a working, so long as there is no creature. All the listed activities exist in God as his nature, not as a kind of reflexive action as when with our fingers we fiddle with something without being aware we are doing so. However, once "creature" or creation enters the picture, the situation becomes different.

And out of this expressing and revealing of himself unto himself, arises the distinction of Persons. As Father he simply abides in observant stillness, touching nothing. As the Son he holds in mind the building patterns of the entire cosmos, gross and subtle, and as the Holy Spirit he responds to those patterns and manifests them. Thus it is.

> But when God as God is made man, or where God dwells in a godly man, or one who is "made a partaker of the divine nature," in such a man somewhat appertains unto God which is his own, and belongs to him only and not to the creature. And without the creature, this would lie in his own Self as a Substance or wellspring, but would not be manifested or wrought out into deeds.

Just as man cannot become God (though he can become god), neither can God become man even though he dwells in a perfected human being. Therefore even in a state of union with God, God holds to what is proper to him, and the human in whom he dwells holds to what is proper to him. They do not become confused or mingled. Their distinction is always clear. When God "acts" in a man, that man is involved in it. Which is why Saint Paul says we are "workers together with him" (II Corinthians 6:1; I Corinthians 3:9).

> Now God will have it to be exercised and clothed in a form, for it is there only to be wrought out and executed. What else is it for? Shall it lie idle? What then would it profit? As good were it that it had never been; nay better, for what is of no use exists in vain, and that is abhorred by God and Nature.

The divine will or pattern is being spoken of here. When God touches a man and begins to work in him then all of the divine plan is revealed in him. This is the particular function of God the Son or Ishwara. And it is impossible for this working to not take place and eventually complete itself. The One Life manifests in all creation, "for the earnest expectation of the creature [creation] waiteth for the manifestation of the sons of God" (Romans 8:19).

Nothing "exists in vain." It is impossible. Everything is as it should be and shall remain so.

However God will have it wrought out, and this cannot come to pass (which it ought to do) without the creature. Nay, if there ought not to be, and were not this and that–works, and a world full of real things, and the like,–what were God himself, and what had He to do, and whose God would He be?

The important concept here is the fact that we are intended to be "workers together" with God, that we are an integral part of the evolution of the cosmos. This really is only logical since we are even now the sons of God, made in the divine image.

> Finish, then, your new creation;
>   pure and spotless let us be;
> Let us see your great salvation
>   perfectly restored in thee:
> Changed from glory into glory,
>   till in heaven we take our place,
> Till we cast our crowns before thee,
>   lost in wonder, love and praise.

Here we must turn and stop, or we might follow this matter and grope along until we knew not where we were, nor how we should find our way out again.

Otherwise we may go beyond our capacity and get lost in speculation rather than insight.

In the Light of God

(Chapter Thirty Two)

In short, I would have you to understand, that God (in so far as He is good) is goodness as goodness, and not this or that good.

God is the Good, the True and the Beautiful. He is also Goodness, Truth and Beauty. Yet there is not a thing that we can indicate and correctly say: "That is God," meaning that it is the totality of God. Everything is God and nothing is God. There we have it. God is the Supreme Attainment, the Paramartha. Yet we really cannot say anything about God that can reveal his essence. God is beyond the intellect, but not beyond the divine spirit in each one of us. It is possible to unite with God, to know God. But the result will be silence, divine silence.

But here mark one thing. Behold! what is sometimes here and sometimes there is not everywhere, and above all things and places; so also, what is to-day, or to-morrow, is not always, at all times, and above all time; and what is some thing, this or that, is not all things and above all things.

Now behold, if God were some thing, this or that, He would not be all in all, and above all, as He is; and so also, He would not be true Perfection.

Therefore God is, and yet He is neither this nor that which the creature, as creature, can perceive, name, conceive or express.

Therefore if God (in so far as He is good) were this or that good, He would not be all good, and therefore He would not be the One Perfect Good, which He is.

This should be read very carefully and thoughtfully. If it seems difficult to understand or even to be incomprehensible that is because of the grave intellectual and spiritual deficiency which has been a trait of the West from the beginning. Only in the East will we find the key; only as yogis will we be able to comprehend, and then ourselves embody the truth of God, for the truth of God and man is the same thing. God is inseparable from man and man is inseparable from God. But only through yoga does it make any sense in a practical manner.

Now God is also a Light and a Cognition, the property of which is to give light and shine, and take knowledge; and inasmuch as God is Light and Reason, He must give light and perceive.

God is both Illuminator and the Illumined. He alone reveals himself. It is his nature to communicate himself to man. If someone has any other purpose in seeking God, his life is in vain. People have created endless rewards or blessings that God is supposed to bestow, but that is superstition and the greed of deluded humanity. The one thing God has to offer us is himself, just as the one thing we have to offer God is our life in Ishwara-pranidhana—offering of the life to God.

And all this giving and perceiving of light exists in God without the creature; not as a work fulfilled, but as a substance or well-spring.

To reveal himself is innate in God. It is what he does. And our purpose in existing is to experience that revelation and know God—and ourselves in God.

But for it to flow out into a work, something really done and accomplished, there must be creatures through whom this can come to pass.

We are the work of God. The entire cosmos is a stage for the drama of creation, of evolution and liberation. We are the sole purpose of creation, therefore the realization of God is our sole purpose, even though nearly the whole human race is throwing its life away in vanities and mirages.

Look you: where this Reason and Light is at work in a creature, it perceives and knows and teaches what itself is; how that it is good in itself and neither this thing nor that thing.

Reading this I recalled a neighbor talking about the difference between well-to-do children and her children. "Rich kids and rich adults, too, think that they can't do a thing if they don't take classes to learn how. For example, lots of the children here took horse-riding classes. My kids wanted to ride, so they just jumped on a horse and rode away!" Some years before this I had looked over a cold-type machine to use in our monastery's publications. When I asked the salesman what instruction I would need, he smiled and said: "I can show you in forty-five minutes everything you need to know. But we offer a course lasting seven evenings for secretaries because they don't believe they can work with the machine without hours and hours of instruction. They aren't stupid; they are just brainwashed." When I picked up a device meant for calculating how to set the dials on the machine, he laughed outright and said: "That's just a girlie gadget. Even a grade-school child can do the calculations in their head. But they think they can't, so they don't."

This is a definite effect of modern life and the dependence on gadgetry. In spiritual matters it is even more pronounced. No one believes they can just start moving toward God on their own. They think that someone must show them every step of the way. This is especially true regarding yoga. They think that they can't make any spiritual progress without a guru, and even accept the ridiculous idea that it is better to not even try to meditate if you do not have a guru.

The Frankfurter tells us that it is God's nature to lead and illumine those who want to draw close to God. The idea that God will bless us to do spiritual practice, but will not teach or bring the teaching to us in some outer form is silly. Everyone accepts the story from the Mahabharata that Arjuna made an image of Drona and learned archery from it, but they balk when it comes to interior development. Jesus said: "It is written in the prophets, And they shall be all taught of God. Every man therefore that hath heard, and hath learned of the Father, cometh unto me" (John 6:45).

> **This Light and Reason knows and teaches men, that it is a true, simple, perfect Good, which is neither this nor that special good, but comprehends every kind of good.**

Amazing: God can speak for himself!

> **Now, having declared that this Light teaches the One Good, what does it teach concerning it? Give heed to this. Behold! even as God is the one Good and Light and Reason, so is He also Will and Love and Justice and Truth, and in short all virtues.**

The How To and the Why To can be learned from God or from saints and angels he sends to help the questing soul. As Yogananda said: "This one thing I have learned in my life: God never forsakes the devotee." As the song says: "Just trust him and be true, and see what he will do."

> **But all these are in God one Substance, and none of them can be put in exercise and wrought out into deeds without the creature, for in God, without the creature, they are only as a Substance or well-spring, not as a work.**
>
> **But where the One, who is yet all these, lays hold of a creature, and takes possession of it, and directs and makes use of it, so that He may perceive in it somewhat of his own, behold, in so far as He is Will and Love, He is taught of Himself, seeing that He is also Light and Reason, and He wills nothing but that One thing which He is.**

Our reason for existing is to be taught by God, and God's reason for bringing us forth into relative existence was so he could teach us. We have the same purpose. Even if we have forgotten it, God has not.

> Behold! in such a creature, there is no longer anything willed or loved but that which is good, because it is good, and for no other reason than that it is good, not because it is this or that, or pleases or displeases such a one, is pleasant or painful, bitter or sweet, or what not. All this is not asked about nor looked at.

God is loved because he is God. That is the sum and substance of true devotion.

> And such a creature does nothing for its own sake, or in its own name, for it has quitted all Self, and Me, and Mine, and We and Ours, and the like, and these are departed.

Ego is gone and God alone remains, both as himself and the divine image in the devotee.

> It no longer says, "I love myself, or this or that, or what not." And if you were to ask Love, "What lovest you?" she would answer, "I love Goodness." "Wherefore?" "Because it is good, and for the sake of Goodness."

We do not love God for what he does, but for what he *is*.

> So it is good and just and right to deem that if there were ought better than God, that must be loved better than God. And thus God loves not Himself as Himself, but as Goodness. And if there were, and He knew, ought better than God, He would love that and not Himself. Thus the Self and the Me are wholly sundered from God, and belong to Him only in so far as they are necessary for Him to be a Person.

So it is.

> Behold! all that we have said must indeed come to pass in a Godlike man, or one who is truly "made a partaker of the divine nature;" for else he would not be truly such.

So the Teutonic Knight has shown us great things and shown us how to evaluate ourselves as seekers after God. Countless people throughout the world are utterly self-deceived in spiritual matters. But they would not be if they would study the Bhagavad Gita and the *Theologia Germanica*.

THE WAY OF DIVINE LOVE

(CHAPTER THIRTY THREE)

One of the essentials of yoga practice according to the sage Patanjali is swadhyaya: self analysis leading to self-understanding. We should continually be checking our state of mind and life against the words and examples of the truly enlightened masters of all ages. Otherwise we may become deluded as to our true spiritual status. This is simple, blessed truth which we should take very seriously when considering our inner and outer life. In the subsequent chapters of *Theologia Germanica* the characteristics of those who truly dwell in non-dual consciousness are outlined so we can compare them with our present status and see what more we need to ensure our perfection in God. Sometimes the author uses the kind of expressions we are used to hearing from contemporary Churchianity, but if we consider them in their higher meaning it will be useful to us.

> **Hence it follows, that in a truly Godlike man, his love is pure and unmixed, and full of kindness, insomuch that he cannot but love in sincerity all men and things, and wish well, and do good to them, and rejoice in their welfare.**

We easily toss around the terms "image" and "likeness" regarding the innate nature of man in relation to God. But we do not usually give any thought to what we are saying, and we certainly have no expectation that a godly person will be exactly as the Priest-knight describes.

There is no denying that such a person is extremely rare, even in India where the guru usually moves around exuding a kind of tranquil absent-though-present atmosphere which the disciples consider the presence of God. Since the guru must appear detached, his relations and reactions to others are markedly pastel in character. Actually the more absent-though-present he can appear, the more surely he will be considered of an exalted non-dual status, mercifully remaining here with mortals out of compassion when he could be in the higher worlds where he belongs.

But the author is exactly right in the way he describes a truly holy person. There are such wondrous souls, though they are rare. Swami Sivananda was exactly as the Frankfurter describes. He was the embodiment of loving-kindness of the most personal kind. As Swami Chidananda once said in a talk about Sivananda, his every thought day and night was how to help others more. Sivananda did not love humanity in an abstract way, he loved every single individual in a deeply personal way.

> Yes, let them do what they will to such a man, do him wrong or kindness, bear him love or hatred or the like, yea, if one could kill such a man a hundred times over, and he always came to life again, he could not but love the very man who had so often slain him, although he had been treated so unjustly, and wickedly, and cruelly by him, and could not but wish well, and do well to him, and show him the very greatest kindness in his power, if the other would but only receive and take it at his hands.

Here are two examples.

One evening in the Sivanandashram satsang hall the lights had been turned out and all were meditating. Suddenly there came a tremendous crash. When the lights were switched on everyone saw that an insane man had tried to kill Sivananda with an axe, and had barely missed his head and driven the axe blade into the wall. Some of the ashramites took hold of the man and led him away. The satsang resumed, led by Sivananda who was totally calm. When the satsang ended, he pulled the axe out of the wall and went to where the man was being kept. He had everyone stand back. Then he handed the axe to the man, folded his hands and said: "If I have done you any wrong, you may strike me." The man did nothing. Then Sivananda told him: "You are still welcome here, and I hope you will stay." The man eventually regained his sanity and with it his ego, so in his embarrassment he decided to leave. Sivananda went with him to the train station and gave him food to eat during the journey, money and other gifts. "Please come back when you feel better," he told the man, "this is your home and you will always have a place here."

For many years during Paramhansa Yogananda's lifetime there was a man who never missed a chance to slander Yogananda. He would do his best to convince people that Yogananda was a fraud and they should have nothing to do with him. He, however, was always around Yoganandaji and the ashram, peeking and poking around to find fault and waiting for his next chance to defame Yogananda. A short time before Yogananda left his body, this man came when some special visitors were there, joining their group as though one of them. When their visit was concluded, Yogananda walked with them down the stairs. On a landing he gently held the man back while the others went on. Yogananda's eyes filled with tears as he said to him: "Please remember this: I will love you always." When he reached his home the man could not forget those words. Suddenly he was filled with remorse for the years he had tried to ruin Yogananda's reputation. For days he was profoundly grieved. Finally he went to the ashram to ask Yogananda's forgiveness. But he found that Yoganandaji had left his body just a few days before. The man vowed that for the rest of his life he would speak well of Yogananda at every chance he got.

Yogananda himself often said that spiritual aspirants should be like roses and sandalwood: the more they are crushed, the more they shed their perfume. As a devotional song to Yogananda I learned on my first trip to India says: "Going far away [from India] you taught dharma. And the dharma you taught you showed perfectly in your life."

> The proof and witness whereof may be seen in Christ; for He said to Judas, when he betrayed Him: "Friend, wherefore art you come?" Just as if He had said: "Thou hatest Me, and art Mine enemy, yet I love thee and am your friend. Thou desirest and rejoicest in My affliction, and do the worst you canst unto Me; yet I desire and wish thee all good, and would fain give it thee, and do it for thee, if you wouldst but take and receive it."

As though God in human nature were saying: "I am pure, simple Goodness, and therefore I cannot will, or desire, or rejoice in, or do or give anything but goodness. If I am to reward thee for your evil and wickedness, I must do it with goodness, for I am and have nothing else." Hence therefore God, in a man who is "made partaker of his nature," desires and takes no revenge for all the wrong that is or can be done unto Him. This we see in Christ, when He said: "Father, forgive them, for they know not what they do."

This is the truth absolute. Not the lies about God's justice being outraged and how he made Jesus a sacrifice, the innocent for the guilty, though he went ahead and banished the sinners to eternal hell fire anyway. Just as Sivananda thought continually of how he might better serve others, God himself continually works for the eventual salvation of all sentient beings. That is his nature; he cannot do otherwise.

> Great is Thy faithfulness, O God my Father,
> There is no shadow of turning with Thee;
> Thou changest not, Thy compassions, they fail not.
> As Thou hast been Thou forever wilt be.

"Every good gift and every perfect gift is from above, and cometh down from the Father of lights, with whom is no variableness, neither shadow of turning." (James 1:17).

> Likewise it is God's property that He does not constrain any by force to do or not to do anything, but He allows every man to do and leave undone according to his will, whether it be good or bad, and resists none. This too we see in Christ, who would not resist or defend Himself when his enemies laid hands on Him. And when Peter would have defended Him, He said unto Peter: "Put up your sword into the sheath: the cup which My Father has given Me, shall I not drink it?"

Is this the Christianity most people know? Just the opposite. But this is the true Christianity. Here we have a Roman Catholic priest writing eight hundred years ago exactly what a yogi in India would have written on the same subject. Jesus spent over half of his life in India before returning to Israel and teaching there what he had learned in India. After the religious authorities tried to kill him he returned to India and lived there for the rest of his life. (See *The Christ of India*.)

Neither may a man who is made a partaker of the divine nature, oppress or grieve any one. That is, it never enters into his thoughts, or intents, or wishes, to cause pain or distress to any, either by deed or neglect, by speech or silence.

Consider how coercive and even vicious Churchianity has been throughout the centuries in dealing with those who do not accept the brazen lies and superstitions they call Christianity. They have not hesitated to kill thousands and destroy entire civilizations. That itself proves that they are not of God but of Satan. If you have ever been ganged up on by "believers" you know what I mean. When I think of the dire prophecies made by the unrighteous as to how God would smite me eventually for not following their ways, I can laugh. But it was no fun at the time. They were themselves a scourge, but not from God.

The Way of Divine Humility

(Chapter Thirty Five)

In a man who is made a partaker of the divine nature, there is a thorough and deep humility, and where this is not, the man has not been made a partaker of the divine nature.

As I said at the beginning of the preceding chapter, this is simple, blessed truth which we should take very seriously when considering our inner and outer life.

So Christ taught in words and fulfilled in works. And this humility springs up in the man, because in the true Light he sees (as it also really is) that Substance, Life, Perceiving, Knowledge, Power, and what is thereof, do all belong to the True Good, and not to the creature; but that the creature of itself is nothing and has nothing, and that when it turns itself aside from the True Good in will or in works, nothing is left to it but pure evil.

There is only the One Absolute. If we attempt to turn away from that Sole Reality, where will we go? There is nowhere to go. Therefore we turn to nothing, to emptiness, and in time become ourselves empty nothingness–dead in the only sense that it is possible for us to be. "For my people have committed two evils; they have forsaken me the fountain of living waters, and hewed them out cisterns, broken cisterns, that can hold no water" (Jeremiah 2:13). But for those who turn to God, there "shall flow rivers of living water" (John 7:38). With God it truly is All Or Nothing.

> And therefore it is true to the very letter, that the creature, as creature, has no worthiness in itself, and no right to anything, and no claim over any one, either over God or over the creature, and that it ought to give itself up to God and submit to Him because this is just. And this is the chiefest and most weighty matter.

If we truly realize this, then divine humility will arise spontaneously. And if we hold on to this insight, it will remain with us always.

> Now, if we ought to be, and desire to be, obedient and submit unto God, we must also submit to what we receive at the hands of any of His creatures, or our submission is all false.

This is an extremely drastic attitude for human beings to adopt. It was, however, the way of Saint John Maximovitch of Shanghai and San Francisco. He would resist or answer no lies spread about him, however slanderous. On occasion he simply ignored the actions of those around him and remained centered within. This caused many people to think that he colluded with evildoers, and he was even brought into court and accused of collaborating with criminals in their wrongdoing because he lived according to the foregoing words of the priest-knight.

Many saints have refused to defend themselves and therefore been judged guilty. More than one holy woman, disguising herself as a monk to escape those who would prevent her from leading a monastic life, was accused of fathering a child and adjudged guilty because she would not deny the falsehood.

In the twentieth century Bishop Charles W. Leadbeater was accused wildly of various forms of immorality and even of propagating them. He never at any time defended or denied in self-defense, so even today there are those who spew out accusations against him that have never been substantiated. Recently I came across a website that has fabricated accusations that were never made during his lifetime. But even if he were here, he would simply go about his Father's business and leave his enemies to their antics. Why would a person choose to do this? Because of the conviction that the universe originates in God and the hand of God should be seen in all things. Therefore if the good and pleasant are accepted in life, so also must the evil and painful be accepted.

There is a story known throughout India about a saint who considered that everything which happened to him was the will of Ram–of God. Here is how Sri Ramakrishna relayed it:

"In a certain village there lived a very pious weaver. Everyone loved and trusted him. The weaver used to go to the market to sell his cloths. If a customer asked the price of a piece of cloth, he would say: 'By the will of Rama, the thread costs one rupee; by the will of Rama, the labour costs four annas; by the will of Rama, the profit is two annas; by the will of Rama the price of the cloth as it stands is one rupee and six annas.' People used to have such confidence in him that they would immediately pay the price and take the cloth.

"The man was a true devotee. At night after supper he would sit for a long time and meditate on God and repeat His holy Name. Once it was late in the night. The weaver had not yet gone to sleep. He was sitting alone in the courtyard near the entrance, smoking. A gang of robbers was passing that way. They wanted a porter and seeing this man, they dragged him away with them. Then they broke into a house and stole a great many things, some of which they piled on the poor weaver's head. At this moment the watchman came. The robbers at once ran away, but the poor weaver was caught with his load. He had to spend that night in confinement.

"Next morning he was brought before the magistrate. The people of the village, hearing what had happened, came to see the weaver. They unanimously declared, 'Your Honor, this man is incapable of stealing anything.' The magistrate then asked the weaver to describe what had occurred. The weaver said: 'Your Honor, by the will of Rama, I was sitting in the courtyard. By the will of Rama, it was very late in the night. By the will of Rama, I was meditating upon God and repeating His holy Name. By the will of Rama, a band of robbers passed that way. By the will of Rama, they dragged me away with them. By the will of Rama, they broke into a house. By the will of Rama, they piled a load on my head. By the will of

Rama, I was caught. Then by the will of Rama, I was kept in prison and this morning I am brought before your Honor.' The magistrate, seeing the innocence and spirituality of the man, ordered him to be acquitted. Coming out, the weaver said to his friends, 'By the will of Rama, I have been released.'

"Whether you live in the world or renounce it, everything depends upon the will of Rama. Throwing your whole responsibility upon God, do your work in the world."

A devotee of Anandamayi Ma and a dear friend of mine, Mr. Haridutta Vasudev, told me that he grew up with his parents having sadhus living in the house. One very memorable sadhu was simply called Ram Bhagat–Devotee of Rama. He was a man of total simplicity. Whenever he went out from the house, dishonest people would come to him and say: "I want…," and name something he had, including his clothing. He would immediately give to them whatever they wanted. Often he returned to the Vasudev house without shoes and without clothing except for his kaupin (underwear.) Naturally the family was annoyed that unscrupulous people would take such advantage of the sadhu's nature and rob him. (They were not annoyed with Ram Bhagat: they revered him all the more.) So they would demand: "Ram Bhagat, who took your shoes, who took your clothes?" Always he replied: "Ram took them." "No, some human being took your things. Who was it?" they would object. Always the answer was the same: "Ram did it." The children were not as reserved as their parents and used to threaten: "Ram Bhagat! Tell us who did this or we will tickle you." And they would. He was very ticklish and sometimes even fell on the floor and rolled around laughing. Finally he would gasp out: "All right. I will tell you! I will tell you!" They would stop, and he would jump up and run out the door, shouting: "Ram did it!" And that was how things always went. Such are the saints.

Anandamayi Ma also considered that everything that happened to her came from God. Once when I was with Ma in Brindaban a Tantric magician sneaked into Ma's room one afternoon when everyone was resting. When some of those who travelled with her came into the room, he was sitting there making gestures (mudras) at Ma and pronouncing curses. Ma was sitting watching him with apparently great interest. When he saw the other people enter he got up and ran out of the building. One of the devotees told me about it soon after and said: "We are very worried, because Ma never rejects anything." And they were right to worry, because in a few days Ma was unconscious and looked nearly dead. In time she came back to normal, but until then it was not a happy time.

Sivananda was the same. People used to come to the ashram with their families to have a free vacation with free food. Every day they would roam the ashram and find new visitors and fill their ears with slanders about Swami Sivananda. He knew they did it, but saw them as God and never objected. This and his loving treatment of the insane man that tried to kill him during the satsang prove the truth of his autobiographical poem: "Only God I Saw."

> From this latter article flows true humility, as indeed it does also from the former. And unless this verily ought to be, and were wholly agreeable to God's justice, Christ would not have taught it in words, and fulfilled it in His life. And herein there is a veritable manifestation of God; and it is so of a truth, that of God's truth and justice this creature shall be subject to God and all creatures, and no thing or person shall be subject or obedient to her.
>
> God and all the creatures have a right over her and to her, but she has a right to nothing: she is a debtor to all, and nothing is owing to her, so that she shall be ready to bear all things from others, and also if needs be to do all things for others. And out of this grows that poorness of spirit of which Christ said: "Blessed are the poor in spirit" (that is to say, the truly humble), "for theirs is the Kingdom of Heaven." All this has Christ taught in words and fulfilled with His life.

In his incarnation as David, Jesus had written: "They also that seek after my life lay snares for me: and they that seek my hurt speak mischievous things, and imagine deceits all the day long. But I, as a deaf man, heard not; and I was as a dumb man that openeth not his mouth. Thus I was as a man that heareth not, and in whose mouth are no reproofs. For in thee, O Lord, do I hope: thou wilt hear, O Lord my God. (Psalms 38:12-15). (For information on Jesus' prior incarnations see *Robe of Light*.) Then as Jesus he followed perfectly the same ideal:

"And they that had laid hold on Jesus led him away to Caiaphas the high priest, where the scribes and the elders were assembled..... Now the chief priests, and elders, and all the council, sought false witness against Jesus, to put him to death.... And the high priest arose, and said unto him, Answerest thou nothing? what is it which these witness against thee? But Jesus held his peace. And the high priest answered and said unto him, I adjure thee by the living God, that thou tell us whether thou be the Christ, the Son of God. Jesus saith unto him, Thou hast said.... Then the high priest rent his clothes, saying, He hath spoken blasphemy; what further need have we of witnesses? behold, now ye have heard his blasphemy. What think ye? They answered and said, He is guilty of death. Then did they spit in his face, and buffeted him; and others smote him with the palms of their hands, saying, Prophesy unto us, thou Christ, Who is he that smote thee?" (Matthew 26:57, 59, 62-68).

"And Jesus stood before the governor: and the governor asked him, saying, Art thou the King of the Jews? And Jesus said unto him, Thou sayest. And when he was accused of the chief priests and elders, he answered nothing. Then said Pilate unto him, Hearest thou not how many things they witness against thee? And he answered him to never a word; insomuch that the governor marvelled greatly" (Matthew 2711-14).

As Isaiah Jesus had prophesied of himself: "He was oppressed, and he was afflicted, yet he opened not his mouth: he is brought as a lamb to the slaughter, and as a sheep before her shearers is dumb, so he openeth not his mouth" (Isaiah 53:7).

Such conduct and outlook can only arise from perfect realization of non-dual Reality.

What Sin Really Is

(Chapter Thirty Six)

> **Further you shall mark: when it is said that such a thing or such a deed is contrary to God, or that such a thing is hateful to God and grieves His Spirit, you must know that no creature is contrary to God, or hateful or grievous unto Him, in so far as it is, lives, knows, has power to do, or produce ought, and so forth, for all this is not contrary to God.**

People who live in a coarse or brutish environment grow up speaking and acting in a coarse or brutish manner. Unfortunately, in the scriptures of Western religions words are put into the mouth of God and his prophets that are nothing less than indecent, scurrilous, violent, sadistic and hateful. Often God sounds more like an out-of-control monster. This is because the authors of such unholy books are projecting their own evil onto God. For it is a universal folly for human beings to create God in their own image.

So the Priest wants us to know that such language as he cites is utterly alien to God and the godly. And never should it be listened to. Since God is love (I John 4:8, 16) and there is no shadow of turning with him (James 1:17), he cannot by his very nature do anything but love all beings.

How the Priest dealt with his own Church we do not know. I expect it was very quietly and cautiously.

> **That an evil spirit, or a man is, lives, and the like, is altogether good and of God; for God is the Being of all that are, and the Life of all that live, and the Wisdom of all the wise; for all things have their being more truly in God than in themselves, and also all their powers, knowledge, life, and the rest; for if it**

were not so, God would not be all good; And thus all creatures are good. Now what is good is agreeable to God, and He will have it. Therefore it cannot be contrary to Him.

Since existence within relativity is the projection of God, and since every sentient being has existed eternally in the depths of God's Being, everything is good with the Goodness of God.

But what then is there which is contrary to God and hateful to Him? Nothing but Sin. But what is Sin? Mark this: Sin is nothing else than that the creature wills otherwise than God wills, and contrary to Him. Each of us may see this in himself; for he who wills otherwise than I, or whose will is contrary to mine, is my foe; but he who wills the same as I, is my friend, and I love him. It is even so with God: and that is sin, and is contrary to God, and hateful and grievous to Him. And he who wills, speaks, or is silent, does or leaves undone, otherwise than as I will, is contrary to me, and an offence unto me. So it is also with God: when a man wills otherwise than God, or contrary to God, whatever he does or leaves undone, in short all that proceeds from him, is contrary to God and is sin. And whatsoever Will wills otherwise than God, is against God's will. As Christ said: "He who is not with Me is against me." Hereby may each man see plainly whether or not he be without sin, and whether or not he be committing sin, and what sin is, and how sin ought to be atoned for, and wherewith it may be healed. And this contradiction to God's will is what we call, and is, disobedience. And therefore Adam, the I, the Self, Self-will, Sin, or the Old Man, the turning aside or departing from God, do all mean one and the same thing.

The Greek word translated "sin" is *amartano*, which means to miss the mark, fall short of the mark and thereby fail, or to err in some manner. "Shortcomings" is the English word that best conveys the idea. For sin is both a condition and a mode of action. Because people are in the state of sin, of being less than they should or could be either from ignorance, weakness or willful negativity, they will as a matter of course engage in actions that are sin or sinful. *Amartano* also implies the root word *meros*, which means piece or portion, the idea being something that is incomplete.

The problem is expressed very well in the Confiteor formulated by Bishop James Wedgwood for the Liberal Catholic Mass:

"O Lord, Thou hast created man to be immortal and made him to be an image of Thine own eternity; yet often we forget the glory of our heritage and wander from the path which leads to righteousness. But Thou, O Lord, hast made us for Thyself and our hearts are ever restless till they find their rest in Thee. Look with the eyes of Thy love upon our manifold imperfections and help us to overcome all our shortcomings, that we may be filled with the brightness of the everlasting light and become the unspotted mirror of Thy power and the image of Thy goodness; through Christ our Lord. Amen."

So the solution to the problem is to come up to the mark, to fulfill the purpose of our existence by being filled with the brightness of the everlasting light and becoming the unspotted mirror of divine power and the image of divine goodness.

How In God, As God, There Can Neither Be Grief, Sorrow, Displeasure, Nor The Like, But How It Is Otherwise In A Man Who Is "Made A Partaker Of The Divine Nature."

(CHAPTER THIRTY SEVEN)

In God, as God, neither sorrow nor grief nor displeasure can have place, and yet God is grieved on account of men's sins. Now since grief cannot befall God without the creature, this comes to pass where He is made man, or when He dwells in a Godlike man. And there, behold, sin is so hateful to God, and grieves Him so sore, that He would willingly suffer agony and death, if one man's sins might be thereby washed out. And if He were asked whether He would rather live and that sin should remain, or die and destroy sin by His death, He would answer that He would a thousand times rather die. For to God one man's sin is more hateful, and grieves Him worse than His own agony and death. Now if one man's sin grieves God so sore, what must the sins of all men do? Hereby you may consider, how greatly man grieves God with his sins.

When God dwells in a fully awakened human being who realizes and objectifies his eternal oneness with God, that illumined person both loathes and grieves over the sin he encounters in humanity. He does not loathe or grieve over the sinner, but over the terrible, destructive effects that sin has on that hapless individual. His loathing and grief arise from love for that person and from his awareness of that person's innate divine nature which is meant to be manifest. For he sees the suffering and confusion which sin is producing in him, and will continue producing until sin is erased from him.

Toward the end of his ministry: "When Jesus was come near, he beheld the city [Jerusalem], and wept over it, saying, If thou hadst known, even thou, at least in this thy day, the things which belong unto thy peace! but now they are hid from thine eyes. For the days shall come upon thee, that thine enemies shall cast a trench about thee, and compass thee round, and keep thee in on every side, and shall lay thee even with the ground, and thy children within thee; and they shall not leave in thee one stone upon another; because thou knewest not the time of thy visitation" (Luke 19:41-44). Jesus is not fulminating or cursing, but grieving because he knows the effect of the people's rejection. Just as when crucified he prayed: "Father, forgive them; for they know not what they do" (Luke 23:34). His thought and care was for them, not himself. So it always is with the truly perfect. Love, not ego, is the source of such reactions.

> And therefore where God is made man, or when He dwells in a truly Godlike man, nothing is complained of but sin, and nothing else is hateful; for all that is, and is done, without sin, is as God will have it, and is His. But the mourning and sorrow of a truly Godlike man on account of sin, must and ought to last until death, should he live till the Day of Judgment, or for ever. From this cause arose that hidden anguish of Christ, of which none can tell or knows ought save Himself alone, and therefore is it called a mystery.
>
> Moreover, this is an attribute of God, which He will have, and is well pleased to see in a man; and it is indeed God's own,

for it belongs not unto the man, he cannot make sin to be so hateful to himself. And where God finds this grief for sin, He loves and esteems it more than ought else; because it is, of all things, the bitterest and saddest that man can endure.

It is an incredible concept that God "becomes man, when he dwells in a truly godlike man." But so it is, because we are always one with God, drawing our existence from him. We are coeternal with God, living within him with his life. This is hard to conceive well, but it can be realized in the consciousness of a perfect human being, man or woman.

All that is here written touching this divine attribute, which God will have man to possess, that it may be brought into exercise in a living soul, is taught us by that true Light, which also teaches the man in whom this Godlike sorrow works, not to take it unto himself, any more than if he were not there. For such a man feels in himself that he has not made it to spring up in his heart, and that it is none of his, but belongs to God alone.

God loves humanity through his perfected saints (siddhas).

How We Are To Put On The Life Of Christ From Love, And Not For The Sake Of Reward, And How We Must Never Grow Careless Concerning It, Or Cast It Off

(Chapter Thirty Eight)

Now, wherever a man has been made a partaker of the divine nature, in him is fulfilled the best and noblest life, and the worthiest in God's eyes, that has been or can be.

One of my university professors said that he had a tone-deaf friend who had learned to recognize the Star Spangled Banner, so to him music was comprised of only two things: the Star Spangled Banner and everything else. It is the same with cosmic existence. There are two modes of being: relative and transcendent. The transcendent mode has also two modes: Infinite and finite–God and god within God. The first is that of God alone, and the second is that of those who have attained absolute perfection in evolution and therefore have attained perfect Self-realization as finite gods within God, living and participating in the very Being of God as their own essential being. It cannot really be defined or described, but it can be experienced-realized by those who ascend in consciousness to the ultimate height of union with Existence-Knowledge-Bliss Itself: Satchidananda. But there are no two ways about it: either you are There or you are not. There are not degrees: it is all or nothing. (We are never really "nothing," although we may feel and function like it.)

Whether we call it Self-realization or God-realization, it is a state of *consciousness*–not divine grace or blessing or inspiration or devotion or love, but entering into and becoming divine, participating in the divine omnipresence, omnipotence and omniscience. This alone is the goal. Anything less is only a step on the ascending pathway that becomes a trap if it is not gone beyond. Again: All or nothing.

Being a state of consciousness this is primarily an interior condition, though the outer life will definitely manifest the presence of the deified consciousness within the person.

It does not result from "pleasing God," it results from *becoming* god. Partaking of the divine nature is both cause and effect and are inseparable. And those who attain it are not merely godlike, but god.

And of that eternal love which loves Goodness as Goodness and for the sake of Goodness, a true, noble, Christ-like life is so greatly beloved, that it will never be forsaken or cast off.

First of all, it will never be forsaken or cast aside because "whosoever is born [begotten] of God doth not commit sin; for his seed remaineth in him: and he cannot sin, because he is born of God" (I John 3:9). Alchemists could turn base metal into gold, but once that was done, they could not turn that gold back into base metal. The change was irrevocable. In the same way, the deified life cannot be abandoned or set aside because it is the very state of being of the spiritual alchemist.

The life of the deified person is not lived for any purpose whatsoever, however noble or seemingly holy. It is lived because nothing else can be done: it is the very nature of the deified one. Purpose involves desire, but he who has attained the All has fulfilled all possible desire.

Therefore, if a person "falls" from any spiritual state it is because it was not the ultimate state of perfect deification. Very few are there at any time who attain that state. But many are those who ascend very high and sink back to a low level because they did not progress high enough and transcend even "the path" and thereby be "out of the game" entirely and unable to lose that state of being which is their very existence itself. They do not "possess" that state, they ARE that state. They have become transmuted into perfect divinity, even though remaining finite. Again, the transmuted gold cannot become debased.

Those who are on the way to that transmutation must love its prospect so greatly that to turn back is unthinkable, even incomprehensible, to them.

Travel Song

Know you the journey that I take?
Know you the voyage that I make?
The joy of it – one's heart could break.

No jot of time have I to spare,
Nor will to loiter anywhere,
So eager am I to be there

For that the way is hard and long,
For that gray fears upon it throng,
I set my journey to the song.

And it grows wondrous happy so
Singing I hurry on for–oh!
It is to God, to God I go.

Sister Maddaleva

Then in time turning back is no longer possible, for the goal shall have been reached, the journey ended.

Up-Hill

Does the road wind up-hill all the way?
　　Yes, to the very end.
Will the day's journey take the whole long day?
　　From morn to night, my friend.

But is there for the night a resting-place?
　　A roof for when the slow dark hours begin.
May not the darkness hide it from my face?
　　You cannot miss that inn.

Shall I meet other wayfarers at night?
　　Those who have gone before.
Then must I knock, or call when just in sight?
　　They will not keep you standing at that door.

Shall I find comfort, travel-sore and weak?
　　Of labour you shall find the sum.
Will there be beds for me and all who seek?
　　Yea, beds for all who come.

Christina Rossetti

Where a man has tasted this life, it is impossible for him ever to part with it, were he to live until the Judgment Day. And though he must die a thousand deaths, and though all the sufferings that ever befell all creatures could be heaped upon him, he would rather undergo them all, than fall away from this excellent life; and if he could exchange it for an angel's life, he would not.

The secret of perseverance is experiencing the divine life. "O taste and see that the Lord is good" (Psalms 34:8). Then there will be no turning back. For the seeker shall have become the goal.

> This is our answer to the question, "If a man, by putting on Christ's life, can get nothing more than he has already, and serve no end, what good will it do him?" This life is not chosen in order to serve any end, or to get anything by it, but for love of its nobleness, and because God loves and esteems it so greatly.

There are many truly silly reasons given for people's behavior, such as climbing a mountain "because it's there." But the yoga marga, the path to divinization through Self-realization, is taken up because it is literally The Thing To Do since it is the fulfilling of the eternal destiny of every single jivatman. It is not a decision or a command, it is the sole purpose of the individual spirit's existence. It is simply an unfolding of the innate nature of a sentient being. It is undoubtedly very complex in its manifestation-realization, yet it's impetus is totally simple: that is the way it IS. It is without beginning, yet it has an all-embracing Ending. The Goal is conscious union-identity with Brahman, the Ekam, Evam, Adwitiyam: the "One, Only, Without A Second."

A seed does not decide to become a plant. It simply becomes one because it is its inherent nature. And this is true throughout the entire range of evolving life from the lowest to the highest world. It is not just the most natural thing to occur, it is the only destiny any sentient being has. And its realization comes about solely from a profound interior process of awakening, realization and manifestation that is its very essential nature. The only way to understand and accomplish this is the message of the Bhagavad Gita: "Therefore be a yogi" (Bhagavad Gita 6:46). This is the beginning, the middle and the end. All jivas must be self-awakened, self-empowered and self-enlightened: this is Self-Realization.

> And whoever says that he has had enough of it, and may now lay it aside, has never tasted nor known it; for he who has truly felt or tasted it, can never give it up again.

Can you "give up" your heartbeat or your breath? Can you give up your very existence? No. Because it is you yourself, your essence, your very being.

The true spiritual path, the true journey from finite to the Infinite–from the unreal to the Real, from darkness to the Light, from death to Life–cannot be laid aside because it is the inevitable Self-unfolding of each one of us. It is the manifestation-revelation of our Self. We cannot leave this path, this process, anymore than we can go out of existence. It is US.

I would like to point out that those who are really moving forward on this path never consider that they can "go too far" or "do too much" in their ongoing journey. Because they know–and have always known from the first step–that it demands our ALL. Those who do not "lay it all on the line" from the beginning have never entered the path. It is a total commitment to the realization and manifestation of our own Reality. The price is Everything. And those who walk that path know that and desire to pay the price.

> And it grows wondrous happy so
> Singing I hurry on for–oh!
> It is to God, to God I go.

There are no spiritual deadbeats on the true path.

And he who has put on the life of Christ with the intent to win or deserve ought thereby, has taken it up as an hireling and not for love, and is altogether without it. For he who does not take it up for love, has none of it at all; he may dream indeed that he has put it on, but he is deceived.

Christ did not lead such a life as His for the sake of reward, but out of love; and love makes such a life light and takes away all its hardships, so that it becomes sweet and is gladly endured.

"For my yoke is easy, and my burden is light" (Matthew 11:30). The "yoke" spoken of is the yoke which is borne by an ox in plowing a field. For an ox it is light, but it would break the back of a dog. This is the difference between the merely called and the chosen.

"For many are called, but few are chosen" (Matthew 22:14). It is very much like when a notice is given about offered employment. Many may apply, but only the truly qualified will be considered, and out of them only the best will be chosen and engaged. All sentient beings are called. And all in time shall respond and be chosen, but only after they have "ripened" through significant inner evolution. Until then, only the "already 'ready'" ones will be chosen.

How do we know the "chosen"? By their joyful acceptance of the call and their willingness and ability to fulfill all requirements and begin immediately to run the race. They alone will win.

The unworthy and incapable are never truly called and have no business with the path of the chosen. So the priest-knight continues:

> **But to him who has not put it on from love, but has done so, as he dreams, for the sake of reward, it is utterly bitter and a weariness, and he would fain be quit of it. And it is a sure token of an hireling that he wishes his work were at an end. But he who truly loves it, is not offended at its toil or suffering, nor the length of time it lasts.**

"Well, I could never do that," and "God does not expect us to do that" were the common coin of those who had no interest in true spiritual life (to which they were averse) when I was growing up in fundamentalist Protestantism. What they really meant was, "I don't want to do that" because their hearts were closed to real spiritual life and its sacrifices and obligations which they disliked.

Here is what the Gospels tell us:

"And being in Bethany in the house of Simon the leper, as he [Jesus] sat at meat, there came a woman having an alabaster box of ointment of spikenard very precious; and she brake the box, and poured it on his head.

"And there were some that had indignation within themselves, and said, Why was this waste of the ointment made? For it might have been sold for more than three hundred pence, and have been given to the poor. And they murmured against her.

"And Jesus said, Let her alone; why trouble ye her? she hath wrought a good work on me. For ye have the poor with you always, and whensoever ye will ye may do them good: but me ye have not always. She hath done what she could: she is come aforehand to anoint my body to the burying. Verily I say unto you, Wheresoever this gospel shall be preached throughout the whole world, this also that she hath done shall be spoken of for a memorial of her.

"And Judas Iscariot, one of the twelve, went unto the chief priests, to betray him unto them" (Mark 14:3-10).

Earlier at another time according to the Gospel of John: "Then took Mary a pound of ointment of spikenard, very costly, and anointed the feet of Jesus, and wiped his feet with her hair: and the house was filled with the odour of the ointment. Then saith one of his disciples, Judas Iscariot, Simon's son, which should betray him, Why was not this ointment sold for three hundred pence, and given to the poor? This he said, not that he cared for the poor; but because he was a thief, and had the bag, and bare what was put therein" (John 12:3-6).

The very sight of the costly offering of Saint Mary goaded Judas into betraying Jesus. Those who are their own personal Judas–betraying and selling their inner Christ to their lower nature and the love of the world–behave in the same way. And pretend to be very virtuous and wise in doing so.

Sacrifice and dedication in spiritual life are offensive and bitter to those who worship the Satan of the ego. But those that are true of heart follow gladly the example of "Jesus the author and finisher of our faith; who for the joy that was set before him endured the cross, despising the shame, and is set down at the right hand of the throne of God" (Hebrews 12:2). And they shall be enthroned there as well.

Therefore it is written, "To Serve God and live to Him, is easy to him who does it."

It is bitter and despised and denied only by those who refuse to serve and live to God.

Truly it is so to him who does it for love, but it is hard and wearisome to him who does it for hire. It is the same with all

virtue and good works, and likewise with order, laws, obedience to precepts, and the like. But God rejoices more over one man who truly loves, than over a thousand hirelings.

Let us be in that blessed company along with Jesus and his holy ones!

DID YOU ENJOY
READING THIS BOOK?

Thank you for taking the time to read *Christian Non-Dualism.* If you found it meaningful, or if it inspired you, or simply gave you something worth pondering, we invite you to leave a short review on Amazon, Goodreads, or anywhere books are shared.

Word of mouth is one of the greatest gifts you can offer to independent publishers, and helps keep this work in motion.

CONTINUE Your Journey Within:
GET YOUR FREE MEDITATION GUIDE

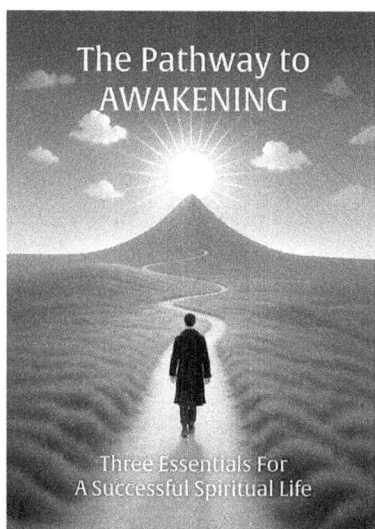

Sign up for the Light of the Spirit Newsletter and get
The Pathway to Awakening: Three Essentials for a Successful Spiritual Life

Get free updates: newsletters, blog posts, and podcasts, plus exclusive content from Light of the Spirit Monastery.

Visit: https://ocoy.org/signup

GLOSSARY

Advaita: Non-dualism; non-duality; literally: not [a] two [dvaita].

Advaita Vedanta: The teaching that there is only One Reality (Brahman-Atman), as found in the Upanishads. Non-dualistic philosophy, especially that of Shankara.

Advaitic: Non-dual; having to do with the philosophy of Advaita (Non-Dualism).

Ahankara: Ego; egoism or self-conceit; the self-arrogating principle "I," "I" am-ness; self-consciousness.

Aishwarya: Dominion, power; lordship; divine glory; majesty; splendor; attribute(s) of Ishwara.

Amrita: That which makes one immortal. The nectar of immortality that emerged from the ocean of milk when the gods churned it.

Atma(n): The individual spirit or Self that is one with Brahman; the essential being, nature or identity of each sentient being.

Avatar(a): A fully liberated spirit (jiva) who is born into a world below Satya Loka to help others attain liberation. Though commonly referred to as a divine incarnation, an avatar actually is totally one with God, and therefore an incarnation of God-Consciousness.

Bhagavad Gita: "The Song of God." The sacred philosophical text often called "the Hindu Bible," part of the epic Mahabharata by Vyasa; the most popular sacred text in Hinduism.

Brahma: The Creator (Prajapati) of the three worlds of men, angels, and archangels (Bhur, Bhuwah, and Swah); the first of the created beings; Hiranyagarbha or cosmic intelligence. See **Kalpa** for an explanation of the Days and Night of Brahma and the length of his term as Creator.

Brahman: The Absolute Reality; the Truth proclaimed in the Upanishads; the Supreme Reality that is one and indivisible, infinite, and eternal; all-pervading, changeless Existence; Existence-knowledge-bliss

Absolute (Satchidananda); Absolute Consciousness; it is not only all-powerful but all-power itself; not only all-knowing and blissful but all-knowledge and all-bliss itself.

Brahmanishtha: Remaining steadfast in the Absolute (Brahman). One who is firmly established in the Supreme being, in the direct knowledge of Brahman, the Absolute Reality.

Brahmastithi (or Brahmistithi): The establishment or dwelling in Brahman.

Buddhi: Intellect; intelligence; understanding; reason; the thinking mind; the higher mind, which is the seat of wisdom; the discriminating faculty.

Chidakasha: "The Space (Ether) of Consciousness (Chit)." The infinite, all-pervading expanse of Consciousness from which all "things" proceed; the subtle space of Consciousness in the Sahasrara (Thousand-petalled Lotus). The true "heart" of all things. Brahman in Its aspect as limitless knowledge; unbounded intelligence. This is a familiar concept of the Upanishads. It is not meant that the physical ether is consciousness. The Pure Consciousness (Chit) is like the ether (Akasha), an all-pervading continuum.

Dharma: The righteous way of living, as enjoined by the sacred scriptures and the spiritually illumined; law; lawfulness; virtue; righteousness; norm.

Dharmi: One who follows dharma.

Dharmic: Having to do with dharma; of the character of dharma.

Ekam-evam-advitiyam: "One, only, without a second." A description of Brahman.

Guna: Quality, attribute, or characteristic arising from nature (Prakriti) itself; a mode of energy behavior. As a rule, when "guna" is used it is in reference to the three qualities of Prakriti, the three modes of energy behavior that are the basic qualities of nature, and which determine the inherent characteristics of all created things. They are: 1) sattwa–purity, light, harmony; 2) rajas–activity, passion; and 3) tamas–dullness, inertia, and ignorance.

Ishwara: "God" or "Lord" in the sense of the Supreme Power, Ruler,

Master or Controller of the cosmos. "Ishwara" implies the powers of omnipotence, omnipresence and omniscience.

Ishwarapranidhana: Offering of the life (prana) to God.

Japa: Repetition of a mantra.

Jiva: Individual spirit.

Jivanmukta: One who is liberated here and now in this present life.

Jivatman: Individual spirit; individual consciousness.

Kalpa: A Day of Brahma–4,320,000,000 years. It alternates with a Night of Brahma of the same length. He lives hundred such years. Brahma's life is known as Para, being of a longer duration than the life of any other being, and a half of it is called Parardha. He has now completed the first Parardha and is in the first day of the second Parardha. This day or Kalpa is known as Svetavarahakalpa. In the Day of Brahma creation is manifest and in the Night of Brahma is it resolved into its causal state.

Karma: Karma, derived from the Sanskrit root kri, which means to act, do, or make, means any kind of action, including thought and feeling. It also means the effects of action. Karma is both action and reaction, the metaphysical equivalent of the principle: "For every action there is an equal and opposite reaction." "Whatsoever a man soweth, that shall he also reap" (Galatians 6:7). It is karma operating through the law of cause and effect that binds the jiva or the individual soul to the wheel of birth and death. There are three forms of karma: sanchita, agami, and prarabdha. Sanchita karma is the vast store of accumulated actions done in the past, the fruits of which have not yet been reaped. Agami karma is the action that will be done by the individual in the future. Prarabdha karma is the action that has begun to fructify, the fruit of which is being reaped in this life.

Krishna: An avatar born in India about three thousand years ago, Whose teachings to His disciple Arjuna on the eve of the Great India (Mahabharata) War comprise the Bhagavad Gita.

Mahashakti: The Great Power; the divine creative energy.

Mantra(m): Sacred syllable or word or set of words through the repetition and reflection of which one attains perfection or realization of the Self. Literally, "a transforming thought" (manat trayate). A mantra, then is a sound formula that transforms the consciousness.

Maya: The illusive power of Brahman; the veiling and the projecting power of the universe, the power of Cosmic Illusion. "The Measurer"–a reference to the two delusive "measures," Time and Space.

Mayic: Having to do with Maya.

Moksha: Release; liberation; the term is particularly applied to the liberation from the bondage of karma and the wheel of birth and death; Absolute Experience.

Mumukshutwa: Intense desire or yearning for liberation (moksha).

Neti-neti: "Not this, not this." The way of describing the indescribable Brahman by enumerating what It is not; the analytical process of progressively negating all names and forms, in order to arrive at the eternal underlying Truth.

Papa(m): Sin; demerit; evil; sinful deeds; evil deeds; trouble; harm; anything which takes one away from dharma.

Papapurusha: Evil personified; personification of the sinful part of the individual.

Paramartha: The highest attainment, purpose, or goal; absolute truth; Reality.

Paramarthika (paramarthic): The Absolute; the absolutely real; in an absolute sense, as opposed to vyavaharika or relative.

Prakriti: Causal matter; the fundamental power (shakti) of God from which the entire cosmos is formed; the root base of all elements; undifferentiated matter; the material cause of the world. Also known as Pradhana. Prakriti can also mean the entire range of vibratory existence (energy).

Pranam: "To bow;" to greet with respect. A respectful or reverential gesture made by putting the hands together palm-to-palm in front of the chest. A prostration before a deity or revered person.

Punya: Merit; virtue; meritorious acts; virtuous deeds. See Apunya.

Punyapurusha: Merit and virtue personified; personification of the virtuous, dharmic part of the individual.

Purna: Full; complete; infinite; absolute; Brahman.

Rajasic: Possessed of the qualities of the raja guna (rajas). Passionate; active; restless.

Ram: A title of Brahman the Absolute. Though sometimes used as a contraction of the name of Rama, many yogis insist that it is properly applied to Brahman alone and employ it as a mantra in repetition and meditation to reveal the Absolute. Interestingly, Ram (Rahm) is also a title of God in Hebrew.

Rama: An incarnation of God–the king of ancient Ayodhya in north-central India. His life is recorded in the ancient epic Ramayana.

Ramakrishna, Sri: Sri Ramakrishna lived in India in the second half of the nineteenth century, and is regarded by all India as a perfectly enlightened person–and by many as an Incarnation of God.

Ramana Maharshi: A great twentieth-century sage from Tamil Nadu, who lived most of his life at or on the sacred mountain of Arunachala in the town of Tiruvannamalai.

Rupa: Form; body.

Samsara: Life through repeated births and deaths; the wheel of birth and death; the process of earthly life.

Samsara chakra: The wheel of birth and death.

Samsari: The transmigrating soul.

Samsaric: Having to do with samsara; involved with samsara; partaking of the traits or qualities of samsara.

Samsarin: One who is subject to samsara–repeated births and deaths–and who is deluded by its appearances, immersed in ignorance.

Samshaya: Doubt; suspicion.

Sanatana: Eternal; everlasting; ancient; primeval.

Sanatana Dharma: "The Eternal Religion," also known as "Arya Dharma," "the religion of those who strive upward [Aryas]." Hinduism.

Sanatana Dharmi: One who both believes in and follows the principles of Sanatana Dharma.

Sattwa: Light; purity; harmony, goodness, reality.

Sattwa Guna: Quality of light, purity, harmony, and goodness.

Sattwic: Partaking of the quality of Sattwa.

Swabhava: One's own inherent disposition, nature, or potentiality; inherent state of mind; state of inner being.

Swadhyaya: Introspective self-study or self-analysis leading to self-understanding. Study of spiritual texts regarding the Self.

Swarupa: "Form of the Self." Natural–true–form; actual or essential nature; essence. A revelatory appearance that makes clear the true nature of some thing.

Swarupajnana: Knowledge which is of the nature of the Self; knowledge of one's essential nature; knowledge of pure consciousness, which is the highest end in life.

Tapa Loka: The world of tapasya; the world beyond rebirth where adept yogis perpetually engage in tapasya (yoga) until they attain liberation and pass upward into Satya Loka, the realm of the liberated ones who know Brahman.

Tapana: Burning; inflaming.

Tapas: See tapasya.

Tapasya: Austerity; practical (i.e., result-producing) spiritual discipline; spiritual force. Literally it means the generation of heat or energy, but is always used in a symbolic manner, referring to spiritual practice and its effect, especially the roasting of karmic seeds, the burning up of karma.

Tapaswi(n): Ascetic; one who is practising Tapas.

Upanishads: Books (of varying lengths) of the philosophical teachings of the ancient sages of India on the knowledge of Absolute Reality. The upanishads contain two major themes: (1) the individual self (atman) and the Supreme Self (Paramatman) are one in essence, and (2) the goal of life is the realization/manifestation of this unity, the realization of God (Brahman). There are eleven principal upanishads: Isha, Kena, Katha, Prashna, Mundaka, Mandukya, Taittiriya, Aitareya, Chandogya, Brihadaranyaka, and Shvetashvatara, all of which were commented on by Shankara, Ramanuja and Madhavacharya, thus setting the seal of authenticity on them.

Viveka: Discrimination between the Real and the unreal, between the Self and the non-Self, between the permanent and the impermanent;

right intuitive discrimination.

Yoga: Literally, "joining" or "union" from the Sanskrit root yuj. Union with the Supreme Being, or any practice that makes for such union. Meditation that unites the individual spirit with God, the Supreme Spirit. The name of the philosophy expounded by the sage Patanjali, teaching the process of union of the individual with the Universal Soul.

ABOUT THE AUTHOR

Swami Nirmalananda Giri (Abbot George Burke) is the founder and director of the Atma Jyoti Ashram (Light of the Spirit Monastery) in Cedar Crest, New Mexico, USA.

In his many pilgrimages to India, he had the opportunity of meeting some of India's greatest spiritual figures, including Swami Sivananda of Rishikesh and Anandamayi Ma. During his first trip to India he was made a member of the ancient Swami Order by Swami Vidyananda Giri, a direct disciple of Paramhansa Yogananda, who had himself been given sannyas by the Shankaracharya of Puri, Jagadguru Bharati Krishna Tirtha.

In the United States he also encountered various Christian saints, including Saint John Maximovich of San Francisco and Saint Philaret Voznesensky of New York.

For many years Swami Nirmalananda has researched the identity of Jesus Christ and his teachings with India and Sanatana Dharma, including Yoga. It is his conclusion that Jesus lived in India for most of his life, and was a yogi and Sanatana Dharma missionary to the West. After his resurrection he returned to India and lived the rest of his life in the Himalayas.

He has written extensively on these and other topics, many of which are posted at OCOY.org.

ATMA JYOTI ASHRAM
(LIGHT OF THE SPIRIT MONASTERY)

Atma Jyoti Ashram (Light of the Spirit Monastery) is a monastic community for those men who seek direct experience of the Spirit through yoga meditation, traditional yogic discipline, Sanatana Dharma and the life of the sannyasi in the tradition of the Order of Shankara. Our lineage is in the Giri branch of the Order.

The public outreach of the monastery is through its website, OCOY.org (Original Christianity and Original Yoga). There you will find many articles on Original Christianity and Original Yoga, including *The Christ of India*. *Foundations of Yoga* and *How to Be a Yogi* are practical guides for anyone seriously interested in living the Yoga Life.

You will also discover many other articles on leading an effective spiritual life, including *Soham Yoga: The Yoga of the Self* and *Spiritual Benefits of a Vegetarian Diet*, as well as the "Dharma for Awakening" series—in-depth commentaries on these spiritual classics: the Bhagavad Gita, the Upanishads, the Dhammapada, the Tao Teh King and more.

You can listen to podcasts by Swami Nirmalananda on meditation, the Yoga Life, and remarkable spiritual people he has met in India and elsewhere, at http://ocoy.org/podcasts/

Join over 33,000 subscribers and watch over 300 videos on these topics and more, including recordings of online satsangs where Swami Nirmalananda answers various questions on practical aspects of spiritual life. A new series of talks on the Bhagavad Gita has also been added.

Visit our Youtube channel here:
Youtube.com/@lightofthespirit

Reading for Awakening

Light of the Spirit Press presents books on spiritual wisdom and Original Christianity and Original Yoga. From our "Dharma for Awakening" series (practical commentaries on the world's scriptures) to books on how to meditate and live a successful spiritual life, you will find books that are informative, helpful, and even entertaining.

Light of the Spirit Press is the publishing house of Light of the Spirit Monastery (Atma Jyoti Ashram) in Cedar Crest, New Mexico, USA. Our books feature the writings of the founder and director of the monastery, Swami Nirmalananda Giri (Abbot George Burke) which are also found on the monastery's website, OCOY.org.

We invite you to explore our publications in the following pages.

Find out more about our publications at
lightofthespiritpress.com

BOOKS ON MEDITATION

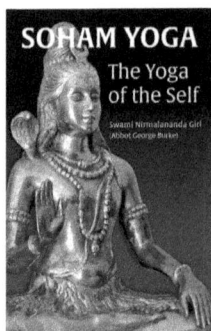

Soham Yoga
The Yoga of the Self

A complete and in-depth guide to effective meditation and the life that supports it, this important book explains with clarity and insight what real yoga is, and why and how to practice Soham Yoga meditation.

Discovered centuries ago by the Nath yogis, this simple and classic approach to self-realization has no "secrets," requires no "initiation," and is easily accessible to the serious modern yogi.

Includes helpful, practical advice on leading an effective spiritual life and many Illuminating quotes on Soham from Indian scriptures and great yogis.

"This book is a complete spiritual path." –Arnold Van Wie

Light of Soham
The Life and Teachings of Sri Gajanana Maharaj of Nashik

Gajanan Murlidhar Gupte, later known as Gajanana Maharaj, led an unassuming life, to all appearances a normal unmarried man of contemporary society. Crediting his personal transformation to the practice of the Soham mantra, he freely shared this practice with a small number of disciples, whom he simply called his friends. Strictly avoiding the trap of gurudom, he insisted that his friends be self-reliant and not be dependent on him for their spiritual progress. Yet he was uniquely able to assist them in their inner development.

The Inspired Wisdom of Gajanana Maharaj
A Practical Commentary on Leading an Effectual Spiritual Life

Presents the teachings and sayings of the great twentieth-century Soham yogi Gajanana Maharaj, with a commentary by Swami Nirmalananda.

The author writes: "In reading about Gajanana Maharaj I encountered a holy personality that eclipsed all others for me. In his words I found a unique wisdom that altered my perspective on what yoga, yogis, and gurus should be.

"But I realized that through no fault of their own, many Western readers need a clarification and expansion of Maharaj's meaning to get the right understanding of his words. This commentary is meant to help my friends who, like me have found his words 'a light in the darkness.'"

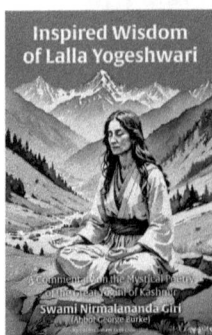

Inspired Wisdom of Lalla Yogeshwari
A Commentary on the Mystical Poetry
of the Great Yogini of Kashmir

Lalla Yogeshwari was a great fourteenth-century yogini and wandering ascetic of Kashmir, whose mystic poetry were the earliest compositions in the Kashmiri language. She was in the tradition of the Nath Yogi Sampradaya whose meditation practice is that of Soham Sadhana: the joining of the mental repetition of Soham Mantra with the natural breath.

Swami Nirmalananda's commentary mines the treasures of Lalleshwari's mystic poems and presents his reflections in an easily intelligible fashion for those wishing to put these priceless teachings on the path of yogic self-transformation into practice.

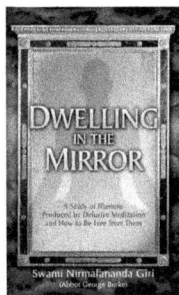

Dwelling in the Mirror
A Study of Illusions Produced By Delusive Meditation
And How to Be Free from Them

Swami Nirmalananda says of this book:

"Over and over people have mistaken trivial and pathological conditions for enlightenment, written books, given seminars and gained a devoted following.

"There are those who can have an experience and realize that it really cannot be real, but a vagary of their mind. Some may not understand that on their own, but can be shown by others the truth about it. For them and those that may one day be in danger of meditation-produced delusions I have written this brief study."

BOOKS ON YOGA & SPIRITUAL LIFE

An Eagle's Flight
A Yogi's Spiritual Autobiography

Swami Nirmalananda Giri shares with rare honesty the struggles, insights, and blessings that have shaped his spiritual life.

Written with his usual insight, vividness, and humor, this book presents stories of his encounters with Anandamayi Ma, Swami Sivananda of Rishikesh and many other saints and yogis.

Satsang with the Abbot
Questions and Answers about Life, Spiritual Liberty,
and the Pursuit of Ultimate Happiness

The questions in this book range from the most sublime to the most practical. "How can I attain samadhi?" "I am married with children. How can I lead a spiritual life?" "What is Self-realization?" "How important is belief in karma and reincarnation?"

In Swami Nirmalananda's replies to these questions the reader will discover common sense, helpful information, and a guiding light for their journey through and beyond the forest of cliches, contradictions, and confusion of yoga, Hinduism, Christianity, and metaphysical thought.

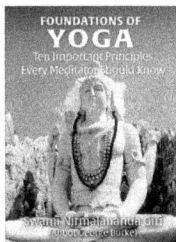

Foundations of Yoga
Ten Important Principles Every Meditator Should Know

An introduction to the important foundation principles of Patanjali's Yoga: Yama and Niyama

Yama and Niyama are often called the Ten Commandments of Yoga, but they have nothing to do with the ideas of sin and virtue or good and evil as dictated by some cosmic potentate. Rather they are determined by a thoroughly practical, pragmatic basis: that which strengthens and facilitates our yoga practice should be observed and that which weakens or hinders it should be avoided.

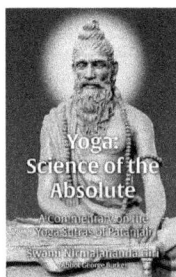

Yoga: Science of the Absolute
A Commentary on the Yoga Sutras of Patanjali

The Yoga Sutras of Patanjali is the most authoritative text on Yoga as a practice. It is also known as the Yoga Darshana because it is the fundamental text of Yoga as a philosophy.

In this commentary, Swami Nirmalananda draws on the age-long tradition regarding this essential text, including the commentaries of Vyasa and Shankara, the most highly regarded writers on Indian philosophy and practice, as well as I. K. Taimni and other authoritative commentators, and adds his own ideas based on half a century of study and practice. Serious students of yoga will find this an essential addition to their spiritual studies.

The Benefits of Brahmacharya
*A Collection of Writings About the Spiritual,
Mental, and Physical Benefits of Continence*

"Brahmacharya is the basis for morality. It is the basis for eternal life. It is a spring flower that exhales immortality from its petals." Swami Sivananda

This collection of articles from a variety of authorities including Mahatma Gandhi, Sri Ramakrishna, Swami Vivekananda, Swamis Sivananda and Chidananda of the Divine Life Society, Swami Nirmalananda, and medical experts, presents many facets of brahmacharya and will prove of immense value to all who wish to grow spiritually.

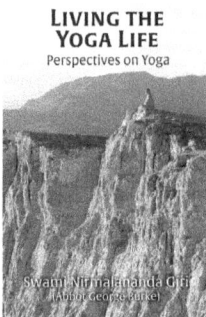

Living the Yoga Life
Perspectives on Yoga

"Dive deep; otherwise you cannot get the gems at the bottom of the ocean. You cannot pick up the gems if you only float on the surface." Sri Ramakrishna

In *Living the Yoga Life* Swami Nirmalananda shares the gems he has found from a lifetime of "diving deep." This collection of reflections and short essays addresses the key concepts of yoga philosophy that are so easy to take for granted. Never content with the accepted cliches about yoga sadhana, the yoga life, the place of a guru, the nature of Brahman and our unity with It, Swami Nirmalananda's insights on these and other facets of the yoga life will inspire, provoke, enlighten, and even entertain.

Spiritual Benefits of a Vegetarian Diet

The health benefits of a vegetarian diet are well known, as are the ethical aspects. But the spiritual advantages should be studied by anyone involved in meditation, yoga, or any type of spiritual practice.

Diet is a crucial aspect of emotional, intellectual, and spiritual development as well. For diet and consciousness are interrelated, and purity of diet is an effective aid to purity and clarity of consciousness.

The major thing to keep in mind when considering the subject of vegetarianism is its relevancy in relation to our explorations of consciousness. We need only ask: Does it facilitate my spiritual growth–the development and expansion of my consciousness? The answer is Yes.

BOOKS ON THE SACRED SCRIPTURES OF INDIA

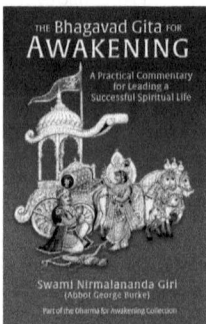

The Bhagavad Gita for Awakening
A Practical Commentary for Leading a Successful Spiritual Life

Drawing from the teachings of Sri Ramakrishna, Jesus, Paramhansa Yogananda, Ramana Maharshi, Swami Vivekananda, Swami Sivananda of Rishikesh, Papa Ramdas, and other spiritual masters and teachers, as well as his own experiences, Swami Nirmalananda illustrates the teachings of the Gita with stories which make the teachings of Krishna in the Gita vibrant and living.

From *Publisher's Weekly*: "[The author] enthusiastically explores the story as a means for knowing oneself, the cosmos, and one's calling within it. His plainspoken insights often distill complex lessons with simplicity and sagacity. Those with a deep interest in the Gita will find much wisdom here."

The Upanishads for Awakening
A Practical Commentary on India's Classical Scriptures

The sacred scriptures of India are vast. Yet they are only different ways of seeing the same thing, the One Thing which makes them both valid and ultimately harmonious. That unifying subject is Brahman: God the Absolute, beyond and besides whom there is no "other" whatsoever. The thirteen major Upanishads are the fountainhead of all expositions of Brahman.

Swamiji illumines the Upanishads' value for spiritual seekers from the unique perspective of a lifetime of study and practice of both Eastern and Western spirituality.

The Bhagavad Gita–The Song of God

Often called the "Bible" of Hinduism, the Bhagavad Gita is found in households throughout India and has been translated into every major language of the world. Literally billions of copies have been handwritten or printed.

The clarity of this translation by Swami Nirmalananda makes for easy reading, while the rich content makes this the ideal "study" Gita. As the original Sanskrit language is so rich, often there are several accurate translations for the same word, which are noted in the text, giving the spiritual student the needed understanding of the fullness of the Gita.

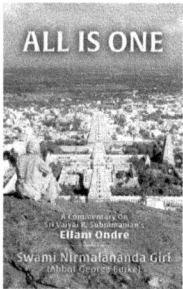

All Is One
A Commentary On Sri Vaiyai R. Subramanian's Ellam Ondre

Swami Nirmalananda's insightful commentary brings even further light to Ellam Ondre's refreshing perspective on what Unity signifies, and the path to its realization.

Written in the colorful and well-informed style typical of his other commentaries, it is a timely and important contribution to Advaitic literature that explains Unity as the fruit of yoga sadhana, rather than mere wishful thinking or some vague intellectual gymnastic, as is so commonly taught by the modern "Advaita gurus."

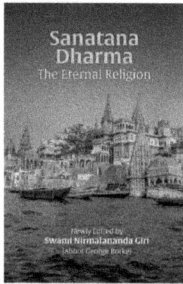

Sanatana Dharma
The Eternal Religion

Sanatana Dharma, commonly called Hinduism, is not just beautiful temples, colorful festivals, gurus and unusual beliefs. It is, simply put, "The Way Things Are" on a cosmic scale. It is the facts of existence and transcendence.

Swami Nirmalananda has edited for the modern reader a book originally printed nearly one hundred years ago in Varanasi, India, for use as a textbook by students of Benares Hindu University. Its original title was *Sanatana Dharma, An Advanced Text Book of Hindu Religion and Ethics*.

A Brief Sanskrit Glossary
A Spiritual Student's Guide to Essential Sanskrit Terms

This Sanskrit glossary contains full translations and explanations of hundreds of the most commonly used spiritual Sanskrit terms, and will help students of the Bhagavad Gita, the Upanishads, the Yoga Sutras of Patanjali, and other Indian scriptures and philosophical works to expand their vocabularies to include the Sanskrit terms contained in these, and gain a fuller understanding in their studies.

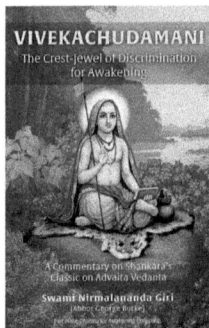

Vivekachudamani The Crest-Jewel of Discrimination For Awakening
A Commentary on Shankara's Classic on Advaita Vedanta

Beyond theory, this commentary offers practical insights for those seeking true spiritual growth, making it an essential guide for both beginners and advanced practitioners of Vedanta.

Whether you are a seasoned yogi or new to the path of spiritual awakening, this book will illuminate your journey, helping you discern the path to higher awareness amidst the clutter of modern spiritual clichés.

Dive into this classic text reimagined for contemporary seekers and transform your understanding of self and reality.

BOOKS ON ORIGINAL CHRISTIANITY

The Christ of India
The Story of Original Christianity

"Original Christianity" is the teaching of both Jesus and his Apostle Saint Thomas in India. Although it was new to the Mediterranean world, it was really the classical, traditional teachings of the rishis of India that even today comprise the Eternal Dharma, that goes far beyond religion into realization.

In *The Christ of India* Swami Nirmalananda presents what those ancient teachings are, as well as the growing evidence that Jesus spent much of his "Lost Years" in India and Tibet. This is also the story of how the original teachings of Jesus and Saint Thomas thrived in India for centuries before the coming of the European colonialists.

May a Christian Believe in Reincarnation?

Discover the real and surprising history of reincarnation and Christianity.

A growing number of people are open to the subject of past lives, and the belief in rebirth–reincarnation, metempsychosis, or transmigration–is commonplace. It often thought that belief in reincarnation and Christianity are incompatible. But is this really true? May a Christian believe in reincarnation? The answer may surprise you.

"Those needing evidence that a belief in reincarnation is in accordance with teachings of the Christ need look no further: Plainly laid out and explained in an intelligent manner from one who has spent his life on a Christ-like path of renunciation and prayer/meditation."—Christopher T. Cook

The Unknown Lives of Jesus and Mary
Compiled from Ancient Records and Mystical Revelations

"There are also many other things which Jesus did, the which, if they should be written every one, I suppose that even the world itself could not contain the books that should be written." (Gospel of Saint John, final verse)

You can discover much of those "many other things" in this unique compilation of ancient records and mystical revelations, which includes historical records of the lives of Jesus Christ and his Mother Mary that have been accepted and used by the Church since apostolic times. This treasury of little-known stories of Jesus' life will broaden the reader's understanding of what Christianity really was in its original form.

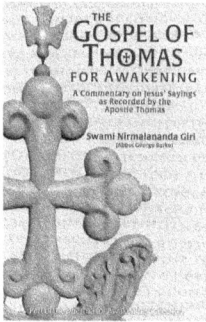

The Gospel of Thomas for Awakening
A Commentary on Jesus' Sayings as Recorded by the Apostle Thomas

When the Apostles dispersed to the various area of the world, Thomas travelled to India, where evidence shows Jesus spent his Lost Years, and which had been the source of the wisdom which he had brought to the "West."

The Christ that Saint Thomas quotes in this ancient text is quite different than the Christ presented by popular Christianity. Through his unique experience and study with both Christianity and Indian religion, Swami Nirmalananda clarifies the sometimes enigmatic sayings of Jesus in an informative and inspiring way.

The Odes of Solomon for Awakening
A Commentary on the Mystical Wisdom of the
Earliest Christian Hymns and Poems

The Odes of Solomon is the earliest Christian hymn-book, and therefore one of the most important early Christian documents. Since they are mystical and esoteric, they teach and express the classical and universal mystical truths of Christianity, revealing a Christian perspective quite different than that of "Churchianity," and present the path of Christhood that all Christians are called to.

"Fresh and soothing, these 41 poems and hymns are beyond delightful! I deeply appreciate Abbot George Burke's useful and illuminating insight and find myself spiritually re-animated." –John Lawhn

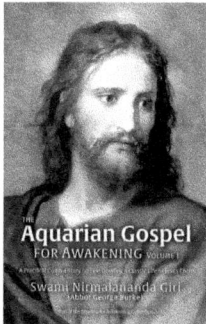

The Aquarian Gospel for Awakening (2 Volumes)
A Practical Commentary on Levi Dowling's Classic Life of Jesus Christ

Written in 1908 by the American mystic Levi Dowling, The Aquarian Gospel of Jesus the Christ answers many questions about Jesus' life that the Bible doesn't address. Dowling presents a universal message found at the heart of all valid religions, a broad vision of love and wisdom that will ring true with Christians who are attracted to Christ but put off by the narrow views of the tradition that has been given his name.

Swami Nirmalananda's commentary is a treasure-house of knowledge and insight that even further expands Dowling's vision of the true Christ and his message.

Robe of Light
An Esoteric Christian Cosmology

In *Robe of Light* Swami Nirmalananda explores the whys and wherefores of the mystery of creation. From the emanation of the worlds from the very Being of God, to the evolution of the souls to their ultimate destiny as perfected Sons of God, the ideal progression of creation is described. Since the rebellion of Lucifer and the fall of Adam and Eve from Paradise flawed the normal plan of evolution, a restoration was necessary. How this came about is the prime subject of this insightful study.

Moreover, what this means to aspirants for spiritual perfection is expounded, with a compelling knowledge of the scriptures and of the mystical traditions of East and West.

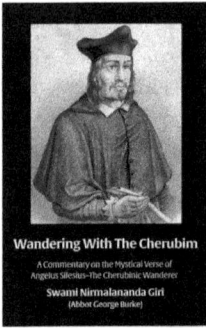

Wandering With The Cherubim
A Commentary on the Mystical Verse of Angelus Silesius–The Cherubinic Wanderer

Johannes Scheffler, who wrote under the name Angelus Silesius, was a mystic and a poet. In his most famous book, "The Cherubinic Wanderer," he expressed his mystical vision.

Swami Nirmalananda reveals the timelessness of his mystical teachings and The Cherubinic Wanderer's practical value for spiritual seekers. He does this in an easily intelligible fashion for those wishing to put those priceless teachings into practice.

"Set yourself on the journey of this mystical poetry made accessible through this very beautifully commentated text. It is text that submerges one in the philosophical context of the Advaita notion of Non Duality. Swami Nirmalananda's commentary is indispensable in understanding higher philosophical ideas, for Swami's language, while readily approachable, is rich in deep essence of the teachings."–Savitri

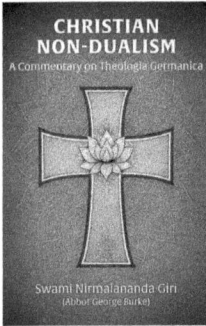

Christian Non-Dualism
A Commentary on Theologia Germanica

What if the roots of Christian mysticism held teachings as profound as those found in the East? What if a single medieval text, long forgotten by mainstream theology, offered a clear and proven path to inner union with God?

Christian Non-Dualism is a revelatory commentary on *Theologia Germanica*, a 14th-century mystical masterpiece that has gone through nearly 200 editions but is almost unknown today. With depth, clarity, and spiritual authority, Swami Nirmalananda Giri unveils the text's rich insights into ego-surrender, divine grace, and the path to inner revelation.

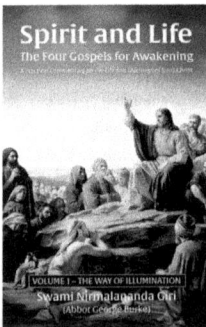

Spirit & Life–The Four Gospels for Awakening
A Practical Commentary on the Life and Teachings of Jesus Christ

Spirit & Life offers a powerful, practical commentary on a harmony of the Gospels, and is not a mere biography but a spiritual revelation consisting of both the life and the teachings of Jesus.

Far from being a conventional or doctrinal study, this book invites readers into the inner life of the soul, where Jesus is not only the Master Teacher, but the awakened Self within. With clarity and reverence, the author examines the inner meaning of the canonical Gospels, unveiling their universal message of illumination, liberation, and union with God.

A two volume set, beautifully illustrated.

BOOKS ON BUDDHISM & TAOISM AND MORE

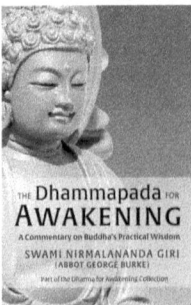

The Dhammapada for Awakening
A Commentary on Buddha's Practical Wisdom

Swami Nirmalananda's commentary on this classic Buddhist scripture explores the Buddha's answers to the urgent questions, such as "How can I find find lasting peace, happiness and fulfillment that seems so elusive?" and "What can I do to avoid many of the miseries big and small that afflict all of us?" Drawing on his personal experience, the author sheds new light on the Buddha's eternal wisdom.

"Swami Nirmalananda's commentary is well crafted and stacked with anecdotes, humor, literary references and beautiful quotes from the Buddha. I have come to consider it a guide to daily living." –Rev. Gerry Nangle

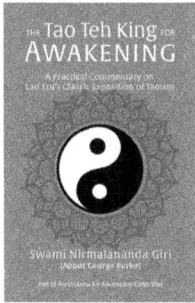

The Tao Teh King for Awakening
A Practical Commentary on Lao Tzu's Classic Exposition of Taoism

"The Tao does all things, yet our interior disposition determines our success or failure in coming to knowledge of the unknowable Tao."

Lao Tzu's classic writing, the *Tao Teh King*, has fascinated scholars and seekers for centuries. Swami Nirmalananda offers a commentary that makes the treasures of Lao Tzu's teachings accessible and applicable for the sincere seeker.

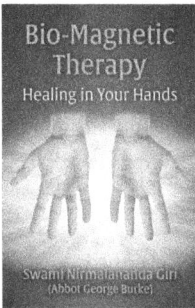

Bio-Magnetic Therapy
Healing in Your Hands

In *Bio-Magnetic Therapy* Swami Nirmalananda teaches the techniques to strengthen your vitality and improve the body's natural healing ability in yourself and in others with specific methods that anyone can use.

Bio-Magnetic Therapy is a simple and natural way to increase the flow of life-force into the body for general good health and to stimulate the supply and flow of life-force to a troubled area that has become vitality-starved through some obstruction. It does not cure; it simply aids the body to cure itself by supplying it with curative force.

How to Read the Tarot
A Practical Method Using the Rider-Waite Deck

Discover Swami Nirmalananda's unique method of reading the Tarot specifically for use with the Rider-Waite deck, with detailed instructions on how to use the cards to develop your intuition for understanding the meanings of the cards. Illustrated with color plates of each of the cards of the Rider-Waite deck with full explanations of their symbolism.

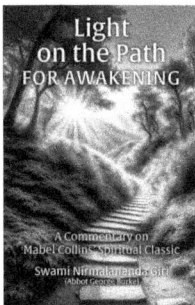

Light on the Path for Awakening
A Commentary on Mabel Collins' Spiritual Classic

In the last quarter of the nineteenth century, Mabel Collins printed a small book on the beginnings of the spiritual quest entitled Light On The Path. She did not consider herself the author but only the transmitter.

This commentary carefully analyzes her transcription, for those who would make the Great Journey must know both the path and how to travel upon it.

Light on the Path explains the nature of discipleship and the qualities of a worthy disciple. The master of such a disciple is the disciple's own divine Self which draws its existence from the Supreme Self: God.

More Titles
Light from Eternal Lamps
Psychic Defense for Yogis